No Man Can Hinder Me

Civil Rights Milestones before 1960

Gregory Salvatore Scime
Edited by: Linda Truillo

ISBN: 1-4802-0163-4
ISBN-13: 9781480201637

Table of Contents

Introduction

When Barack Obama raised his hand in 2009 to take the presidential oath of office there were no eyebrows raised over the fact that he was obviously not 100 percent white.

As he stood on the West Front of the U.S. Capital, he did not appear out of place even when he and Chief Justice John Roberts had trouble getting the words in the right order.

Many people want to take credit for building the road that brought Barack Obama, the first African American, to the Oval Office of the Whitehouse. However, the road was built before anyone realized where it was heading. It was built by people who were far removed from the field of politics and social justice; many of whom today are not around to witness the culmination of their vision.

By the time Barack Obama was born, in 1961, the road was just about completed. The Civil Rights Act of 1964 simply gave the road a name. Historians probably would not agree with my analysis. But I am describing the people and events that made civil rights a reality before it became a law.

Most of the events and the people involved that are described in these chapters are well known and have already been written about in many books. What I have tried to do is point out how these events and these people affected the heart and soul of America. The people I have written about somehow knew that morality was something that required action, not legislation. They somehow knew that morality can not be obstructed. They somehow knew that their efforts could not be hindered.

The courage and vision of black and white Americans, working together in three major areas of American life—music, sports, the armed forces—set an example and a precedent for successful integration throughout all areas of life in America.

Because of the efforts and wisdom of dedicated Americans, black and white, the United States can make a claim that no other nation can. It completely transformed itself in less than one hundred and fifty years—from a racially divided society to a more integrated one. Having waged a revolution to establish its independence, the United States continued fight to defend liberty began with the most successful civil war the world has seen. It was a war in which the victors and the defeated united to form one union. Then followed a century-long parade of people whose love of their country and love of their fellow man enabled them to instinctively know what they needed to do to make America and the world a better place.

The Civil War eliminated slavery. It did not eliminate discrimination, bigotry, prejudice, hatred, and mistrust.

The civil rights movement of the 1960s eliminated some of the remaining areas of discrimination in the workplace and civic life. It did not eliminate bigotry, prejudice, hatred, and mistrust. These feelings had been gradually eroding among most Americans, black and white, over a long stretch of time by the examples of courage, character, patriotism, vision, and wisdom of people of both colors who worked together. It is no small miracle that a group of people, most of whose names are not in any book on the history of civil rights, were able to change feelings that war and political activism could not affect. These feelings of prejudice and bigotry were so embedded in 1860 that hundreds of thousands of southern soldiers were willing to die to preserve them. The Civil Rights movement of the 1960s can claim many victories. But it cannot claim that the movement did anything to change the way people felt about race. If anything, the movement may have temporarily rekindled some negative feelings.

The main reason the civil rights movement had any success at all should be attributed to what was accomplished prior to 1960 by the people described in this book. Without making or breaking any laws, Americans, black and white, famous and not famous, changed people's hearts. Without going to war, without violence, without anger, without riots or demonstrations these people accomplished what laws cannot accomplish, and allowed Americans the opportunity to experience racial harmony before most were even aware of what was happening around them.

Chapter 1
"No Man Can Hinder Me"

The Power of Music among African American Slaves

Ride on, King Jesus!
No man can hinder me
Ride on King Jesus!
No man can hinder me

Jesus rides on a milk white horse
No man can hinder me
The river Jordan he did cross
No man can hinder me

If you want to find your way to God
No man can hinder me
The gospel highway must be trod
No man can hinder me

I was young when I begun
No man can hinder me
But now my race is almost run
No man can hinder me

Gregory Salvatore Scime

"Negro spirituals" are religious songs composed by African Americans, or their descendants, who lived in the United States during the period of slavery. The composers were usually illiterate and have remained anonymous. These songs were primarily expressions of the slave's new found religion, Christianity.

The lyrics to one Negro spiritual begin with the words "Ride on King Jesus. No man can hinder me." The composer of this spiritual was most likely someone born into slavery, and most likely unable to commit these words to paper. But someone did come along at a later time and wrote them down along with the melody to which they were probably sung. By identifying himself with Jesus, the slave gave his life meaning. The author of the lyrics knew that despite his enslaved existence no one could prevent him from doing the right thing and ultimately attain his goal, heaven. The song, with its powerful message, has endured for more than 150 years.

In the early and mid-20th century Negro spirituals were an integral part of the African- American church music repertoire. The choirs of many black churches, especially in the Northeast, regularly performed elaborate arrangements of spirituals as well as classically composed anthems, hymns, and music in the African American gospel style (distinguished from Southern gospel hymns such as "Amazing Grace" or "His Eye Is on the Sparrow.")

As musicologists know well, the message in a Negro spiritual is often double sided: on the one hand it can seem like a simple religious plea as found in the spiritual "Steal

Away," while on the other hand, it can convey an underlying message of hope and even determination. As most of the older African Americans know, the hidden message in the song "Steal Away" refers to escape. A song such as this was often sung when someone in a slave community was planning to run away, often via the "underground railroad." It might even have been sung when a group of slaves were planning to sneak into the woods at the end of the workday to sing and pray, out of sight and out of earshot of the "masters."

Christianity was introduced to black slaves with the hope that they would derive from Christianity a message of submission. However, those who thought this to be true did not understand the full message of the teachings of Christ. Those who were enslaved were able to hear and sense a message more profound than the words seemed to convey. In the stories from the Hebrew Scriptures and in the teachings of Jesus they found a message of liberation of the soul, a hunger to be free in body, and a trust that Jesus would empower them.

Fortunately, for many African Americans, during the time of slavery and the years that followed, the words "No Man Can Hinder Me" resonated within them. The placement of the words within the song disguises its hidden meaning. These words may have empowered many people who could otherwise have felt that their goals for any significant success in life were impossible in the face of racial prejudice as it persisted in America after emancipation. And if they did not hear these words directly, or have the opportunity to decipher for themselves the hidden meanings, African Americans often were taught by their parents and grandparents in a variety of ways that "no man can hinder you." As a response to the obvious barriers of discrimination, African Americans who were exposed to the wisdom of these words developed strong self-confidence.

For an African American living one hundred or more years ago, it could be said that whatever may have seemed impossible in the real world became totally possible when expressed in song. Music was, and continues to be, where truth is found. A wonderful example of this is the message of the hymn "We Shall Overcome."

Within the music of African Americans—whether it be classical, jazz, blues, gospel, soul or spirituals—is contained the total African American experience; and all things are possible if they are expressed in Song.[1] We believe what we sing when the words and the music come from the heart.

By the time the fourth generation of freed blacks were learning "Ride on, King Jesus! No man can hinder me," they were beginning to see the truth of these words through the events that had taken place and were continuing to unfold in the "real world."

Chapter 2
"There's Only One Train upon This Track"

From the First Black University to the Pullman Porters
Every time I feel the spirit moving in my heart I will pray.
There's only one train upon this track. It runs to Heaven and right back

The Civil War eliminated slavery but it did not eliminate prejudice toward blacks. Nor did the war create an America where freed slaves were free in their pursuit of happiness.

At the end of the Civil War in 1865 freed slaves faced new problems. Among the most important of these was that basic education was not being provided to them. Former slaves were not in a position to educate themselves, but it was understood among blacks and their advocates that education was going to be imperative for their economic success. The first attempt to create a school to address this situation was the establishment of Fisk University in Nashville, Tennessee.

Barely six months after the end of the Civil War, and just two years after the Emancipation Proclamation, three white men, John Ogden, the Reverend Erastus Milo Cravath, and the Reverend Edward P. Smith, established the

Fisk School in Nashville, named in honor of General Clinton B. Fisk of the Tennessee Freedmen's Bureau.[2] It was General Fisk who provided the new institution with facilities in former Union Army barracks near the present site of Nashville's Union Station.

In these facilities Fisk convened its first classes on January 9, 1866. The first students ranged in age from seven to seventy, but shared the common experiences of slavery and poverty—and a desire to learn. Many of the first students had limited previous education. Some were completely illiterate. Within a few months enrollment at Fisk reached nine hundred students.

No provisions had been planned for the retraining of freed slaves to enable them to work in areas other than agriculture. Schools like Fisk were among the first to recognize that freed slaves needed basic education in "reading, writing and arithmetic" if they were to be able to survive in their new life-style.

It was a common belief at that time that blacks did not have sufficient intelligence to be educated. Therefore many people honestly assumed that it was a waste of everyone's time to attempt to educate blacks. Some actually thought that it was unfair to black persons to mislead them into believing that they could be educated.

It took men and women of extraordinary vision and selfless character to devote their lives to the task. They were not influenced by popular belief, or, more accurately, by popular misconception. They were very familiar with the stories of struggle and success that were found in the Bible.

The work of Fisk's founders was sponsored by the American Missionary Association,[3] a group that later became part of the United Church of Christ, with which Fisk University retains an affiliation today. Ogden, Cravath, and Smith, along with others in their movement, shared a dream of an educational institution that would be open to all, regardless of race, and that would measure itself by "the highest standards, not of Negro education, but of American education at its best." Their dream was incorporated as Fisk University on August 22, 1867.[4]

The founding of Fisk was one of the first collaborations between blacks and whites to address and solve a problem; not the problem of integration, nor the problem of prejudice or equal rights, but the problem of education. These men and women had the innate wisdom to see the immediate problem. They knew that no one could hinder them from accomplishing their goal, which was the education of newly freed slaves.

Early in its history Fisk University ran into serious financial problems that threatened to close the school. Again, blacks and whites worked together to solve this problem and save the school from extinction, this time with the help of George White, a white Northern missionary who served as the treasurer of the school and as the director of its choir. White had been a first sergeant in the Union Army during the Civil War, but his true vocation was music.

The Fisk choir, which would eventually become the Fisk Jubilee Singers, was a relatively small group of black students, men and women, who happened to have a large talent for singing.[5] In 1871 George White came up with the idea to raise money for the university by taking the choir on a tour of fund-raising concerts. Working together, White and Ella Shepard, one of the singers, organized a concert tour for the choir in hopes of receiving donations. The efforts were not very successful in the beginning. But with the determination of its director and the willingness of the singers to push themselves beyond human limits, the choir eventually raised enough money to save the university, and even expand its facilities. Their efforts resulted in performances at the White House for President Ulysses Grant, and in London for the Queen of England.

In the beginning White had the choir performing a program of European-style classical music. Although the singers were well capable of performing this style of music, audiences were not thrilled. When eventually the choir added what we today refer to as "Negro spirituals" to their programs, they captivated audiences.

White knew the power of music to raise money. And that was his goal. What he may not have anticipated was the power of the music to overcome the seemingly impenetrable wall of racial prejudice and change the hearts of people. Wherever the Fisk singers performed, it was common for them to witness a change of attitude by the white audiences toward their color. Most of the time the changes were small. But it indicated that music was a force that could get past the outer layer of prejudice and touch the soul. Sometimes, however, the changes were not so small.

When the Fisk Jubilee Singers came to New Jersey in 1871 to perform, the administrators of the Newark public schools were so moved by the beauty of their voices and repertoire, which, by this time, comprised primarily arrangements of spirituals, that they voted to allow black students to enter the public schools. This impenetrable wall of segregation in the schools came down without "a mumbling word," (title of a Negro spiritual, *He Never Said a Mumblin' Word"*) and allowed black students the opportunity to disprove the myth that blacks could not be educated nor would they benefit from an education.

That alone would have been a monumental accomplishment. But things didn't stop there. The choir was having major transportation problems as they traveled around the country. Rail travel in the 1870's was the only means of long-distance travel, and, because of discriminatory practices against people of color, black passengers traveled under harsh conditions. At that time, the most luxurious rail accommodations were Pullman sleeper cars, designed by George Pullman, a pragmatic entrepreneur who wanted to sell to the public a means of travel that offered every possible comfort. When Pullman learned that the Fisk Jubilee Singers were traveling under such duress, he, no doubt moved by the beauty of their music and impressed by their determination, gave them a Pullman Sleeper car for their personal use to travel throughout the country to their various concert venues. This can easily be called the first step toward integration of the railroads. The singers were still separated from the white passengers, but they were traveling first class.

The Jubilee Singers did three major fund-raising tours. The third tour began in 1874 with a group of singers twice the size of the original Jubilee Singers. Most of the original nine singers were unable to join the third tour. But the backbone of the group was still George White and Ella Sheppard. Their vision, courage, and determination to build a university were evidence of the truth in the lyrics of the spiritual "No Man Can Hinder Me."

Fisk University and the Fisk Jubilee Singers, through the power of music and the collaboration of blacks and whites, laid the cornerstone of racial integration in two major arenas in the United States, softened the bigotry of a countless number of people, challenged the misconception about the intelligence of blacks, and created a roadmap for the education of millions of African Americans.

As the Jubilee Singers were making inroads in racial acceptance, their benefactor George Pullman was, perhaps without being entirely conscious of it, laying down tracks of his own in the same direction.

It is well known that Pullman was responsible for hiring thousands of former slaves to work as porters on his sleeper cars. Pullman's belief that the type of service he wanted to provide for the sleeper car mode of travel could best be provided by former slaves, and he demanded very high standards of performance from them. Although the job of the Pullman Porter might be considered menial, the men took great pride in their work and were well respected in their communities. With their modest earnings they were usually able to afford nice homes and support their families. Many of them were able to send their children to college. The porters also had the opportunity to travel from one side of the country to the other, gaining a perspective on life that only travel can offer. The job allowed them to see how the rest of the world lived, which was a life-changing experience for men who were born into slavery.

The porters had further evidence that their labor was worth the effort: Frequently, Pullman Porters who left their railroad jobs found excellent positions in first-class hotels and restaurants. Many porters soon were college students themselves working summers to save money for education. In 1912 *The Pullman News* reported that 30 percent of black doctors were former porters. Ultimately, and perhaps most importantly, the tens of thousands of African Americans who worked for George Pullman were able to "set a high standard of dignity" throughout the African American community in all parts of the country. At the same time, Pullman was known for having treated his porters rather harshly. He was accused of overworking and underpaying them. The porters, themselves, complained about working conditions. But, nevertheless, they encouraged their sons and grandsons to follow in their footsteps.

If Pullman is to be judged by the wages he paid the porters, he is probably guilty of violating as-yet unwritten minimum-wage laws. If he is to be judged on his business vision, one that included uneducated and unskilled former slaves, the verdict is quite different.

In his vision for a mode of travel, Pullman had a place for blacks who had been slaves. He saw that they had a unique set of experiences and coping skills that no other business-man at that time could see or use. The high standards he de-manded of his workers bred generations of men who brought those standards back to their communities. Nowhere else, at no other time in the history of America, has any industrial-ist invested his time and money in a project that depended on African Americans for its success. While others may have seen the freed slaves as a burden, Pullman saw them as an asset. While others would never have put their faith in "Ne-groes," Pullman trusted them to succeed. While others were content to ignore the black workforce, Pullman exploited it. While others considered blacks unable to be educated, Pull-man trained them to provide the highest standard of service.

The porters who worked for Pullman were also vision-aries. They saw beyond the low wages and the sometimes menial aspects of their jobs to a respectable place in soci-ety for themselves and future generations of African Ameri-cans. These men knew that through travel they were learn-ing about the world in which they lived. They brought their knowledge and sophistication back to their communities. As a group, the Pullman Porters represented a very early role model for younger African Americans.

A white businessman and an army of black porters helped change and shape America into a better place. Pullman was able to look down the miles of track and realize that there was nothing to prevent him from succeeding. The success he was seeking was not the elimination of prejudice. He never set out to be a humanist. He set out to improve the way people traveled.

It is a phenomenon of biblical magnitude that thousands of African Americans could look down that same stretch of tracks to see a vision for themselves, and were willing to "get on board" and travel the journey. They were not looking to change any laws or complain about their lives. They were concerned with improving their lives and the lives of their families. It's a total mystery, or maybe a miracle, that they sensed that purpose would prevail over prejudice. Without making any laws or breaking any laws George Pullman and the men who worked for him created a middle-class black population.[6]

George Pullman's legacy has its share of blemishes. Whatever the final moral verdict is for him, it cannot be denied that his vision included a group of people who may have had to wait another forty or fifty years for the opportunities he created. While laws have been passed making it illegal to discriminate when hiring, there was no law that required someone to create jobs for a minority group of people. George Pullman was moved by the music of the Fisk singers and not by any laws.

Chapter 3
"Joshua fit the Battle of Jericho, and the walls came a-tumbling down."

African Americans Prove Their Valor in World War I

Perhaps as far back as 1900, shortly after the Spanish American War, many prominent African Americans in New York were anxious to form a Black National Guard Regiment to be based in Harlem. In the beginning of the 20th century the United States depended on state militias, organized as National Guard units, as the primary source of reserve manpower for the armed forces. The State of New York authorized a black guard unit in 1913, but did not provide the means to organize it.[7]

As war raged in Europe during 1914, U.S. President Woodrow Wilson vowed to remain neutral. As the war continued, however, it was apparent that the United States would have to get involved. The imminent war provided the impetus for the government to organize the 15th New York Infantry. Harlem finally had its regiment on June 29, 1916.

Command of the 15th Infantry Regiment was given to a white officer, Colonel William Hayward, by the newly elected Republican Governor of New York, Charles Whitman. Hayward, who was well connected with the governor, also was a veteran of the Spanish American War and had studied with John Pershing as a cadet at the University of Nebraska. Hayward wanted to form the regiment with black officers. As the conflict in France expanded and the United States found itself on the brink of war, the possibility of actually going into battle brought recruitment for the 15th Regiment to a standstill. Although there were many blacks who could meet the qualifications to become officers, there was little interest among them in volunteering. Recruitment of officers in the ranks of enlisted men was equally difficult.

On April 6, 1917, President Woodrow Wilson declared war on Germany. Many of the other regiments in New York were filling with volunteers. The 15th Regiment was not, and so Hayward at first put off his idea of recruiting black officers. He was faced with the decision to nominate experienced white officers or give up the idea of continuing the plan to form any regiment at all. Among the first white officers Hayward chose were Hamilton Fish, a graduate of Harvard, and Lorillard Spencer, a wealthy New Yorker. Both set about actively recruiting black members. Along with the efforts of two black musicians, James Reese Europe and Noble Sissle, the regiment would eventually fulfill its manpower and officer requirements.

When the news came that the Harlem Guard unit would be deployed to France, Colonel Hayward decided that the troops could not be sent overseas without a band. Among the many roles a military band must fulfill, raising morale is primary. Morale is one of the primary factors in maintaining the fighting ability of a soldier. The army therefore decided that a black regiment must have a black band capable of playing a style of music familiar and entertaining to black troops.

One of the popular music styles of the time was this new style that had originated in New Orleans, first called Dixieland, and later New Orleans Jazz. Regardless of what it was called, the music was mostly the creation of black musicians. The army, represented by Colonel Hayward, didn't believe that the white army bands would be capable of entertaining the black troops as well as a black band playing this style of music.

The man selected by Colonel Hayward to form the band was James Reese Europe. Europe was considered to be the most important African American musician in New York at this time. He was the director of the prestigious Clef Club Orchestra. Before Paul Whiteman or George Gershwin were doing it, Europe was presenting jazz concerts in Carnegie Hall. Interestingly, he had already enlisted to serve in the army's 15th Regiment and had been recruiting to fill its ranks. He encouraged other African Americans in Harlem to join, including Nobel Sissle, another prominent black musician, feeling that it would be a great opportunity for young black men to belong to a vibrant social and professional network. At the same time, Europe felt that an all-black regiment would improve the public perception of African Americans. For some reason, however, unknown to his biographers, he enlisted in the army for combat duties, not as a musician. Soon after his enlistment he took and passed the course of study to become a commissioned officer. It has been speculated that Lieutenant Europe had a strong sense of patriotism and wanted to set an example to other blacks.

Before the lieutenant could fulfill his dream of leading a machinegun unit into battle, his (white) commanding officer, Colonel Hayward, convinced him to form an all-black regimental band to accompany the Harlem Guard in France. Hayward told Europe he wanted the "best damn band" in the army. Europe initially did not want to do it. To discourage Colonel Hayward, Lieutenant Europe insisted on conditions that he thought would be impossible for Hayward to deliver.

Originally the army told Europe they wanted the standard twenty-eight-piece band. Europe said he would form a band only if he could have a band of forty-eight musicians. The additional musicians he wanted included cellos and string basses, instruments never before used in a traditional band. Europe also wanted a large amount of money to entice the best black musicians to enlist by offering them a very nice salary. But Hayward miraculously was able to meet all of these demands.

Although he was very surprised and, at the same time, disappointed that Colonel Hayward had somehow come up with the money, Europe began to see this as an opportunity to make the public more aware of black musicians and the quality of their music. It was part of his personality to see opportunity in every situation. His ultimate goal, which he hoped to achieve after the war, was to form a black symphonic orchestra that would perform compositions by black composers. Europe believed that the African race was an integral part of society in America. Although as a black he did not enjoy all the benefits of American life, he somehow knew that democracy had to be preserved—and that the U.S. war effort needed his help—if he was to have the opportunity to pursue his dream.

With the help of Noble Sissle, Lieutenant Europe worked tirelessly to form the band that would accompany the regiment. Europe was well connected in New York music circles. He knew all the best and most popular players. It took James Europe some time to convince forty-eight of the best black musicians to come to the aid of their country. He even traveled to Puerto Rico, where he felt he would find the best woodwind players.

During this time, Europe was informed that he had a life-threatening medical condition requiring immediate surgery: a goiter on his thyroid gland was pressing against his wind pipe causing difficulty in breathing. Refusing to be hospitalized until the band was formed, Europe continued working for many weeks until he could no longer function. In April of 1917 he underwent two surgeries to remove the goiter.

Finally the 15th Regiment had its own band, and it proved to be one of extraordinary talent that would eventually feature the world-famous dancer Bill "Bojangles" Robinson as its drum major.

When the 15th Guard unit arrived in France in 1918 it was renamed the 369th Regiment. The U.S. Army at the time had a strict policy that blacks would serve in segregated units and perform support duties, and would not be allowed to actually participate in combat. Support duties typically included working as stevedores, cooks, drivers, and in other non-skilled capacities behind the battle lines. Such would have been the fate of the 369th Regiment had it not come under the command of General John "Black Jack" Pershing of the American Expeditionary Force.

Pershing got his nick-name, "Black Jack," from his students at the U.S. Military Academy because of his experience commanding black soldiers in the Spanish American War in 1898 and again in 1914, during the Mexican Punitive Expedition. In the first of these conflicts he served with the 10th Cavalry, one of the "Buffalo Soldier" regiments, and became an advocate of African American troops. Pershing did not share the army's opinion that black soldiers couldn't fight and should be relegated to support duties. Pershing believed they were indeed capable and deserving of the opportunity to serve in combat. He was, overall, very concerned about fair treatment for blacks serving in the army, and very likely wanted to see their treatment based on the objective assessment of their character.

Pershing got around the army's policy toward blacks by assigning the 369th to assist the French army. It was the first time American soldiers were commanded by a foreign military. When the French went into combat the 369th went with them. Lieutenant Europe got his chance to be on the front lines in command of a machinegun unit and was injured in a gas attack while serving in combat.

Lieutenant Europe was called back from the front lines, resumed his position as band director, and was given the responsibility of providing entertainment for civilians as well as for the troops and officers. The band performed Europe's original compositions, syncopated arrangements of popular tunes, and his renditions of Sousa marches. The band's concerts captured and held "prisoner" the hearts of American and French soldiers, officers, and French civilians.

When the war ended in late summer of 1918 , Colonel Hayward, or possibly General Pershing, sent Europe and his band on a public relations concert tour to Paris. The band won favor with the French audiences with their renditions of ragtime, jazz, and even marches by John Philip Sousa. Europe had grown up in Washington, D.C., and lived a few doors down from Sousa, who was at that time Commander of the U.S. Marine Band. Europe was given his first music instructions by Enrico Hurlei, Sousa's Assistant Band Director. There can be no doubt that Europe not only knew but also was influenced by Sousa's music. Sousa's Marine Band had already toured France in 1900, and many of the French people remembered his exciting renditions of ragtime music and the marches that Sousa himself composed

The popularity of jazz in France, and in central Europe as well, can definitely be attributed to music of Lieutenant James Reese Europe. It also helps explain why dancer and singer Josephine Baker was so warmly received in Paris six years later without prejudice toward her color.

The troops returned home to a reception far different from their send-off, a welcoming that marked a historic turning point. After the Civil War black soldiers who had fought in the Union Army were not allowed to march in the victory parade along Pennsylvania Avenue in Washington, D.C. When the United States entered World War I black troops of the 15th Regiment from New York (369th) were denied the opportunity to march with the white troops up 5th Avenue in the farewell parade for the New York National Guard Division, known as the Rainbow Division. But when Lieutenant Europe and the Harlem Hellfighters, a name given them by the German soldiers who faced them in battle, returned from France in 1919, they marched right up 5th Avenue to Harlem in a joyous parade with none other than their drum major, Bill "Bojangles" Robinson, leading the way.[8]

The army's policy of segregation had momentarily been stunned by the battlefield achievements of the 369th Regiment, or Hellfighters, and by the members of their Divisional Band. The achievements of the Hellfighters, and five other all-black regiments—the 92nd, 93rd, 370th, 371st, and 372nd—changed the minds and hearts of people in the military and in the civilian world. The moment had come, it seemed, for America to take a second look at its second-class citizens.

And yet, once away from the battlefields and the military parades, the black soldiers returning home found that things in America had not changed as much as they had hoped and expected. Segregation was still legal in many parts of the country, poverty still affected a disproportionate number of black families, and meaningful job opportunities were still scarce for blacks. But, while the country had not changed much, these soldiers had. War had taught them to expect more of themselves and to expect more from the country they had defended.

It was black men of unusual courage who answered the call to serve their country. These men knew that despite their second-class citizenship, America's freedom needed to be defended. They were willing to do this. They knew that service to their country in time of war would inevitably make it impossible for anyone, black or white, to think of African Americas as second-class. These men, though small in number, also had vision. As the historian Barbara Gannon summed it up in her book *The Won Cause*, "Black Americans like James Europe had faith in the notion that military service represented a claim to citizenship and equality."[9]

The courage, patriotism, and fighting ability of the black soldiers, the music of James Reese Europe, as well as the visionary leadership of Colonel Hayward and General John Pershing brought down another section of the seemingly impenetrable wall of prejudice. And in the process, no laws were made or broken.

The breach in the wall, although not immediately apparent, would expand. As black soldiers were breaking a path to social justice, there were some relatively unknown white soldiers who were gearing up to help them. Serving in the Rainbow Division in France during the war were people who later would become very well-known champions of integration; men who served under Pershing and most likely were influenced by the general's respect for the black soldiers; men who probably were eye-witnesses to the valor of their black comrades; men who were probably deeply moved by what they saw. Among these were Major Harry Truman, who later became President, and Major Branch Rickey, the man who would change the color of baseball.

Truman's and Rickey's contributions will be discussed later in this book, but it is worth noting a few facts about Pershing here. This general's role in shaping the American society with regard to racial harmony is rarely recognized because of his stature as one of the country's greatest military leaders. Frank E. Vandiver, author of *Pershing and the Anatomy of Leadership* writes of Pershing in this way:

Pershing was a man of such high moral character that it is not likely that those who served under him were unaffected by his "sensitive humanity," his honesty and his respect for men of all colors.

Vandiver quotes Pershing as saying:

"My attitude toward the Negro, was that of one brought up among them. I had always felt kindly and sympathetic toward them and knew that fairness, justice, and due consideration of their welfare would make the same appeal to them as to any other body of men. Most men, of whatever race, creed, or color, want to do the proper thing and they respect the man above them whose motive is the same. I therefore had no more trouble with the [N]egroes than with any other troops I ever commanded."

From the day the 369th returned to America it took less than thirty years for U.S. military forces to completely desegregate. The desegregation of the military was an across-the-board change of life-style. Every aspect of military life was desegregated, schools on military installations, military hospitals, military housing, military buses, post exchanges (PX), and the list goes on. The military already had one salary scale for all personnel, black or white, which was based on rank and time of service. With desegregation, advancement in rank slowly and surely became a matter of merit.

Pete Nelson, author of *A More Unbending Battle,* writes,

Something new started when the men from Harlem and their black and white officers took up arms and sailed together to France to spend a year that changed the course of American history. The optimists were right—no one could deny them their rights, their country {referring to the enemy abroad}.

At the time, many pessimists believed the racial situation in America could not change. Nelson answers the skepticism:

What the pessimists underestimated was the fight in the men who went away and returned, as well as the pride they would inspire, without which neither battle could be won, the one in France [during World War I] or the one back home.

African Americans who wore the uniform were men who were proud to serve, proud of the country they served, and proud of the officers who led them. In a miraculous way they knew that honor conquers hostility. Pride conquers prejudice. Faith conquers fear.

Chapter 4
"Ain't No Mountain High Enough"

Jazz, Big Bands, and Growing Hopes for Racial Harmony

During the 1920s and 1930s black jazz bands, such as Duke Ellington and Cab Calloway, played to all-white audiences at The Cotton Club in Harlem and the Roseland Ballroom in midtown Manhattan.

Heavyweight boxer Jack Johnson in 1920 opened the Club De Luxe on 142nd Street and Lenox Avenue in Harlem. A bootlegger named Owney Madden took over the club in 1923 and changed the name to The Cotton Club. It was during the period from 1920 to 1933 that the Eighteenth Amendment to the Constitution was in effect prohibiting the sale of alcoholic beverages. The Cotton Club operated during this time selling liquor illegally. Known as "speakeasies" many clubs offered alcoholic beverages and entertainment to entice customers.

During the 1920s and 1930s The Cotton Club was the epitome of the speakeasy. It offered a black-tie environment and entertainment by the best bands in the country. Whites wanting to be chic would travel uptown to Harlem to The Cotton Club to enjoy the best black bands of the time.

At The Cotton Club the lines of segregation were clearly drawn at the edge of the bandstand. The musicians were all black, the audiences were all white.[10] Many of the most important black bands and entertainers built their reputation at The Cotton Club during the years of prohibition. The list of performers reads like a "who's who" in jazz: Count Basie, Duke Ellington, Fletcher Henderson, Ella Fitzgerald, Nat King Cole, Billie Holiday.

But this impenetrable wall of separation was easily penetrated by the music. The black musicians could not mingle with the white patrons of The Cotton Club, and the patrons wouldn't think of crossing the three-hundred-plus-year-old line to socialize with the musicians. But in the 1967 words of a Marvin Gaye song, there "ain't no mountain high enough" that's capable of stopping the flow of communication, and during these years it was music that was going back and forth between the musicians and the audience. Like gamma rays that can pass through almost any substance, the music and the appreciation of the audience flowed back and forth across the invisible line unimpeded by any element of bigotry.

In increments too small to measure every performance at The Cotton Club was building a bridge that would span the chasm that separated the races. Radio waves would extend that bridge clear across the country when the Columbia Broadcasting System began broadcasting from The Cotton Club in 1927. During these days there were no rating services that could determine how many households were tuned into the broadcasts coming from The Cotton Club. By this time almost every American had access to a radio. Therefore it would be safe to say that millions of white Americans had no problem inviting "The Duke" (Duke Ellington) or "The Count" (Count Basie) into their living rooms on a weekly basis. The music was all that mattered.

Big bands were the popular music of the 1920s, 1930s, and 1940s. Bands came in all sizes and styles. There was Louis Armstrong's "Hot Seven" playing a New Orleans' style of jazz and Paul Whiteman's symphonic jazz orchestra. Duke Ellington incorporated classical music elements with jazz, Benny Goodman played a danceable jazz, Count Basie had his Kansas City style, and there were countless other varieties. Through records and radio the American public was tuned into jazz.

In public the white and black musicians did not perform together. But in private, after hours, jazz musicians "jammed" together. The musicians were the first to have their hearts changed by the music. The desire to be with each other and learn from each other created a magnetic attraction that few could resist. It's no secret that white musicians wanted to get closer to black musicians in order to become better jazz musicians.

There is no documentation that clarinetist Benny Goodman and pianist Teddy Wilson ever jammed together.[11] But it wouldn't be far-fetched to imagine that they had. Benny Goodman was born in Chicago in 1909 to Jewish parents who had emigrated from Russia. Teddy Wilson was an African American who was born in Austin, Texas, in 1912. Both men were among the best jazz musicians of the 1930's. Both musicians had light, lyrical styles that worked well together.

Goodman wasn't interested in civil rights or politics. He was one of the top bandleaders in the country and he simply wanted to play with the best musicians. As far as Goodman was concerned, Teddy Wilson was the best pianist for his trio, which included drummer Gene Krupa.[12]

At first the three musicians recorded together. The records were so successful that audiences around the country were requesting appearances by the trio. Black and white musicians were not yet performing together in public, but by popular demand the integrated trio was eventually pressured into doing just that. Although it was the first time the American public had seen integration on the bandstand, you would have needed a micrometer to measure the resistance of the public to this phenomena.

With the later addition of vibraphonist, Lionel Hampton, also African American, the trio became a quartet and changed the world of jazz, and the world, forever.

When they performed together the audiences were interested only in how the music made them feel, not in the skin color of the performers. Working together to make music, Goodman, Wilson, Krupa, and Hampton, The Benny Goodman Quartet, like an erupting volcano, changed the entire landscape in the world of jazz where racial segregation was dying a silent death and was being buried without any mourners. It took the Jazz public no time at all to accept integration on the bandstand. To them the music was more important, more powerful than whatever prejudice they might have had.

One common denominator to a lot of the social progress happening in jazz during the 1930s and 1940s can be attributed to a man by the name of John Henry Hammond. Hammond was born into a very wealthy white family in New York City. He lived on Fifth Avenue in Manhattan and studied classical music at Yale University. Despite his classical music training, Hammond was more interested in the music he was hearing performed by the black servants who worked for his family. From this childhood experience his interest in all styles of music of black Americans was nurtured.

Hammond became the most important talent scout in the field of jazz, having launched the careers of many legendary performers. Hammond was a giant, himself, for his efforts and accomplishments in the racial integration of jazz. His love of the music motivated him to break down the color lines that existed in jazz during the 1930s.

He wasn't satisfied breaking down the internal walls. He was equally motivated to bring the music to a larger audience. To do this he produced a series of concerts in New York's Carnegie Hall.[13] He called the concerts "Spirituals to Swing." Perhaps more than any other person John Hammond is responsible for bringing live jazz to venues that were familiar to larger white audiences. White audiences were get-

Gregory Salvatore Scime

ting used to integrated performances on the most prestigious stage in America. Black musicians were getting used to a sense of pride that goes along with standing center stage at Carnegie Hall.

To the musicians, and the audiences, all that mattered was the music. During the 1930s, as the Great Depression was controlling the economy, the big bands were controlling the mood of the country. There were many things people could not afford during these times, but most people found a way to buy a radio. Night after night they could turn on NBC or CBS and have their spirits lifted by the music of one of the great bands.

The best three of the big bands during the 1930s were Duke Ellington, Count Basie and Benny Goodman (before and after the success of the quartet Goodman fronted several big bands). Count Basie's popularity was the result of the efforts of John Hammond, who heard Basie's band (on the radio) performing in Kansas City. Hammond convinced Basie to come to New York, where the talent scout used his influence to promote the band.

While Basie, Goodman, and Ellington were the giants among big bands, the diminutive drummer, Chick Webb, was leading his own band at the Savoy Ballroom in Harlem. As a result of spinal tuberculosis, Webb was less than five feet tall.

32

No Man Can Hinder Me

As David challenged Goliath, Webb liked to challenge the giants to a "battle of the bands." He invited them to the Savoy Ballroom for the faceoff.

The Savoy was located in Harlem on 140th Street and Lenox Avenue. It was owned by Moe Gale, a Jewish immigrant whose full name was Moses Galewski, and managed by Charles Buchanan, a black real estate broker. It may not have been their intention to create an integrated dance club, but, as intelligent businessmen, they had the common sense to make the dance floor open to everyone regardless of color. Even then, in the 1930s, the Savoy was integrated, integrated to the point where blacks and whites danced with each other. The level of dancing was extraordinary and the competition among the dancers was intense. The power of the music combined with the passion for dancing created an environment of integration at the Savoy that would not have been found anywhere else in the country, perhaps in the world, at that time.

It was an historic event when Goodman's all white big band (not to be confused with Goodman's integrated 4 piece band) showed up at the Savoy to take on the Webb band. Other black bands had entered the battleground at the Savoy. But with Goodman's band it was going to be black versus white. But integration had been internalized into the hearts of the audience. To them the battle of the bands wasn't black versus white. It wasn't about racial pride. It was only about the music. The great "King of Swing," Benny Goodman, was being challenged by the mighty underdog, Chick

Webb. After ballots were cast, the Chick Webb band won. But Goodman remained the "King of Swing."

Thousands of Americans danced their depression troubles away at the Savoy each week. The dancers experienced a totally integrated life style in the middle of Harlem every week for years, thousands of black Americans and white Americans. Everyone who had the opportunity for "Stompin' at the Savoy" learned of the infectious joy of life without prejudice.[14] Among the many dance styles popularized at the Savoy none was more popular than the Lindy Hop.[15]

Although they were not initially interested in eliminating segregation, Buchanan and Gale, the Savoy Ballroom managers, realized over time the importance of what was happening at the Savoy. They continued to work together to bring blacks and whites together. The social impact that the Savoy Ballroom had remains unmeasured. In the world of social change things move slowly, and you can't always know where you're going until you get there.

Along with the Savoy Ballroom, New York's most important concert hall of the 1930's, Carnegie Hall, on 7th Avenue and 57th Street in Manhattan, was another notable venue played by Goodman and his band. When he brought his band to Carnegie Hall in 1938, not only did Goodman introduce jazz to that bastion of classical music, but he also introduced racial integration to the stage of the great hall. Goodman had members of the Duke Ellington and Count Basie bands as featured soloists. What might have been the reaction of the nearly three thousand members of the audience[16] when they saw the integrated collection of musicians on stage having a great time? There can be no doubt that they might have been thinking this racial integration thing looks like it could be a lot of fun. When members of the audience jumped out of their seat to start dancing, could they possibly have had any negative feelings of prejudice in their hearts?

As the Great Depression marched through the 1930s, Americans, black and white, were having their spirits lifted by the music of Basie, Ellington, Goodman, and others like Tommy Dorsey, Louie Armstrong, Ella Fitzgerald, Frank Sinatra, and too many more to mention. Through records and radio the swing era was dancing its way across America with no regard to color. To most Americans nothing was more important or more powerful than the music.

During the height of the depression Americans were tuned into the weekly radio broadcasts from The Cotton Club in New York. Around 1932 Black bandleader Cab Calloway replaced Duke Ellington as the house band of The Cotton Club. The excitement of the music of Calloway's bands, made up of Black musicians, coupled with his energetic showmanship had audiences across the country forgetting their troubles for a few hours a week during the hardest economic times America has ever seen. And for a few hours a week whatever prejudice that may have existed was irrelevant.

Gregory Salvatore Scime

The ability of jazz to influence the country was the result of the numerous big bands being broadcast nationwide by radio and by these same bands touring the United States to perform before audiences from coast to coast. The thousands of venues where jazz could be heard and danced to, and movies featuring well-known jazz musicians further intensified the effect music was having on the nation.

Nobody noticed, but things were changing in the way Americans felt about race. Whites were learning about blacks through music. Blacks musicians were getting used to being taken seriously by white audiences, even if only in performance. Communication was taking place in a way by which neither side felt threatened. People were getting used to integration in a manner so subtle that even Sherlock Holmes could not have detected it. Because it was so subtle, so non-threatening, no one even thought to stop it.

Without making or breaking any laws, black and white jazz musicians came together to bring down a section of the wall separating the races, almost like the biblical walls of Jericho were brought down when Joshua's trumpets started playing. The collaborative efforts of blacks and whites working together produced results neither could have accomplished alone. The integration that began with Benny Goodman and Teddy Wilson changed the American way of living together.

Although Jazz musicians were not on a mission to eliminate segregation, the world of jazz became a testing ground for integration. The jazz world proved that integration works for everybody. It proved that most people have more important things on their minds than prejudice. It proved that the challenge of integration was best handled without attacking it directly. Goodman and Wilson did not get together to improve civil rights. They weren't planning to lobby Congress for legislation. They weren't calling press conferences. They got together to make great music. The rest just followed.

Noted author and jazz saxophonist Steve Lacy was quoted as saying "Risk is at the heart of jazz. Every note we play is a risk." Perhaps it is this attitude that enabled jazz musicians to be first in the world of music to challenge and change the status quo.

Jazz historian Ken Burns said, "I have made a film about jazz that tries to look through jazz to see what it tells us about who we are as a people. I think that jazz is a spectacularly accurate model of democracy and a kind of look into our redemptive future possibilities."

Chapter 5
"In That Great Getting Up Morning"

Marian Anderson's Landmark Performance, Easter 1939

The changes that were taking place in the 1930s musical world of jazz were soon being imitated in the world of classical music.

Marian Anderson was a classically trained African American singer. By 1939 she had successfully toured Europe and the United States. Noted classical pianist Arthur Rubenstein, a Jewish immigrant from Poland, introduced Anderson to Sol Hurok, a Russian Jewish immigrant from the Ukraine. Sol Hurok, the most important impresario in the world, tried to book her into Constitution Hall in Washington, D.C. The DAR (Daughters of the American Revolution), whose membership depended on ancestry, had the authority to bar Marian from performing at Constitution Hall on the basis that black performers were not allowed.

The DAR in this instance exemplified the type of mindless prejudice that some people were able to hold onto. Mindless because, even in 1939, it was already apparent that segregation in the world of music was no longer expected by the general public.

Anderson had already appeared in Carnegie Hall in New York, a venue enormously more important for a musician than Constitution Hall. The DAR must have had their heads in the sand regarding what was going on in the world outside their collective living rooms. How else could they not have anticipated the reaction of the public, especially from one very high-profile member of their own club, Eleanor Roosevelt, wife of President Franklin D. Roosevelt?

The news about the discriminatory attitude of the DAR was front-page news in Washington. Similarly, the city's Board of Education refused the use of a high school auditorium for Anderson's concert. The general public of Washington D.C. reacted to this display of bigotry and committees were formed to protest the decision with citizens picketing the Board of Education offices. The Washington public was generally displeased with the discrimination toward Anderson, as was Eleanor Roosevelt, who on February 26, 1939, resigned from the DAR in protest. In her letter she wrote, "I am in complete disagreement with the attitude taken in refusing Constitution Hall to a great artist … You had an opportunity to lead in an enlightened way and it seems to me that your organization has failed."[17]

As Anderson's manager, Sol Hurok worked with Walter White, the president of the NAACP at that time, and with Eleanor Roosevelt to remedy the situation. Secretary of the Interior Harold Ickes and White had collaborated several years earlier establishing quotas for African American employees in PWA projects. Ickes had also been president of the Chicago NAACP. As Secretary of the Interior he ordered the desegregation of the National Parks, even those in the South. He was determined to arrange a concert for Marian Anderson on the steps of the Lincoln Memorial in Washington, D.C. And he did. On Easter Sunday morning in 1939, 75,000 people showed up to hear Anderson perform. Among the audience were the justices of the Supreme Court and a ten-year-old by the name of Martin Luther King Jr. Millions more heard the concert on radio as it was broadcast across the country.

Anderson began her performance with the song "My Country 'Tis of Thee," followed by several Negro Spirituals, and, though she was not Catholic, the anthem of the Catholic Church, "Ave Maria." In this well-chosen repertoire she demonstrated her patriotism, her sense of the black experience, and her religious faith. And if that were not enough to win every heart, for good measure she added operatic arias.

In attendance at that concert was another black opera singer, Todd Duncan.

In his thirties at the time, he would go on to be the first African America to perform with an all-white cast in a major opera company. He played the role of Tonio in Leoncavallo's *Pagliacci* with the New York City Opera. In a wonderful biography of Anderson by Russell Freedman, Todd Duncan is quoted as saying,

> "My feelings were so deep that I have never forgotten it, and I don't think until I leave this earth will I ever

forget it. Number one, I have never been so proud to be an American. Number two, I have never been so proud to be an American Negro. And number three, I never felt such pride (as) in seeing this Negro woman stand there with this great regal dignity and sing…. The highlight of that day were the first words that she sang."

Those words were "My Country 'tis of Thee."

At the end of the concert Walter White was at the podium, trying to encourage the audience to remain calm, when he spotted a young black girl obviously moved by the experience. Freedman quotes the NAACP president:

Hers was not a face of one who had been the beneficiary of much education or opportunity. Her hands were particularly noticeable as she thrust them forward and upward, trying desperately, though she was some distance from Miss Anderson, to touch the singer…. Tears streamed down the dark girl's face. Her hat was askew, but in her eyes flamed hope bordering on ecstasy. Life, which had not been too easy for her, now held out greater hope because one who was also colored, and who like herself, had known poverty … had, by her genius, gone a long way towards conquering bigotry. If Marian Anderson could do it, the girl's eyes seemed to say, then I can too.

Along with this little girl, there were tens of thousands of people gathered in front of the Lincoln Memorial listening to Anderson on that eventful day. Their very presence insured that there would be no protesters attempting to disrupt the event. (The Ku Klux Klan would never demonstrate where they were outnumbered.) Nor could the millions listening on the radio be disturbed by protesters. What would have been a relatively insignificant concert, had it taken place in Constitution Hall where it was originally planned, became an event of enormous historical importance because a group of people, one black and three whites, would not be hindered. Their goal: let the world hear a great voice. Their accomplishment: another mile of the historic road to integration was paved.

What was accomplished that Easter morning can never be measured. There can be no doubt, however, that across the United States millions of Americans, black and white, were listening to that concert, and for them the great divide between the races was narrowed by a few inches. Anderson's concert didn't convince any prejudiced white person that prejudice is wrong. It merely gave people an opportunity to put prejudice aside for a while. It is very likely that many people went to bed that Sunday night harboring a little less prejudice than they had when they woke up that morning. The spiritual power of music being expressed by a beautiful voice has healing energy to lift the soul.

A few years later even the DAR changed its perspective on race relations and invited Anderson to perform in Constitution Hall to an integrated audience. Music had raised the consciousness of this group of women to enable them to see life from a higher level of morality.

Gregory Salvatore Scime

When Marian put her trust in Sol Hurok, a relationship began that continued for the rest of her career.[18] These two people working together succeeded in presenting to America, in a national broadcast, one of the greatest voices of the century. Instead of trying to break down the door that was closed to them, they looked for another door that wasn't locked. And behind this door was an opportunity that was infinitely more significant than what they originally had in mind. The four main characters in this story—Anderson, Hurok, Roosevelt, and Ickes—used the obstacle put in front of them as a stepping stone.

After the Lincoln Memorial concert It took only sixteen years before the "no colored allowed" sign came down from the stage of the Metropolitan Opera House in New York. In 1955 Marian became the first African American to sing at the Met when she performed the role of Ulrica in Giuseppe Verdi's *Un Ballo in Mascher* (The Masked Ball). The sophisticated Metropolitan Opera audience had already heard Marian's voice in recordings and on radio broadcasts. When the curtain opened on January 7 the audience burst into applause before she sang a note. The love that they felt for the beauty of her voice preceded her arrival. The love they felt for her voice precluded any prejudice. Music had given the audience the opportunity to enjoy the beauty that bigotry excludes.

In 1939 the DAR would not greet Marian Anderson at the front door, or even the back door, of their "elite" club in Washington because she wasn't white. It was only a few months later that Anderson was invited to the White House

44

to sing for the Queen of England. Eighteen years later Marian Anderson was greeted in Washington by President Dwight Eisenhower when she sang for his inauguration. Shortly after that she was greeted by President John Kennedy and sang for his inauguration. And then it was President Lyndon Johnson who invited her to the White House to receive the Presidential Medal of Freedom, the highest award that can be given to a civilian. It is the civilian equivalent to the Medal of Honor, and like the Medal of Honor it is awarded by an act of Congress. Although the members of Congress at the time did not have in their mind any thoughts of passing any serious civil rights legislation, Marian Anderson had quietly changed their hearts.

Without making or breaking any laws, Marion Anderson, with the help of Sol Hurok, Eleanor Roosevelt, and little-known Secretary of the Interior Harold Ickes, also changed the hearts of millions of Americans, black and white, if only a little, about racial relations. When a change starts, however, and it's the right change, like a volcano about to erupt it's impossible to stop it.

Chapter 6
"Take Me Out to the Ballgame"

The Integration of Major League Baseball

When the Boston Braves baseball team moved from Boston to Milwaukee in 1953, the team had already integrated. With the move out of Boston (a city that resisted racial integration), the Braves were less constrained in their choice of players. In 1954 African American Henry (Hank) Aaron joined the team—when Bobby Thomson injured his ankle—and took his position in the outfield. In his first game in the Major Leagues Aaron hit a home run. He continued hitting home runs for the next twenty years. When Aaron hit his 715th, he broke Babe Ruth's record for total home runs. The Atlanta Braves fans held up a sign that read "MOVE OVER BABE."

The record-breaking home run would come in the Braves' opening home game of the 1974 season. The Atlanta Braves, formerly of Milwaukee, were playing the Los Angeles Dodgers, formerly of Brooklyn. During the off-season between 1973 and 1974 Aaron had received a lot of hate mail threatening him with bodily harm if he tried to break Ruth's record. However, the only person who had anything to fear on the first day of baseball in 1974 was Dodger pitcher Al Downing, who was on the mound that day. When Downing looked as if he wasn't going to give Aaron any decent pitches to hit, the crowd began some serious booing. Al Downing felt the pressure and on the next pitch gave Aaron something to hit. When Aaron parked the ball in the bullpen 385 feet from home plate, County Stadium in Atlanta, Georgia, erupted into celebration. But they weren't celebrating a racial event. They were celebrating a baseball event. In 1974 prejudice was no longer a major factor in sports. When the Dodger left fielder, Bill Buckner attempted to climb the fence into the bullpen to retrieve the ball, he was hoping to get his hands on a piece of history and take it home. However, Buckner didn't get to touch it. One of the Altanta Brave pitchers in the bullpen got to the ball first.

Atlanta, Georgia, had been the scene of an important Civil War battle. A hundred years prior to this day, Hank Aaron would not have been able to cast a vote in Atlanta. On this day in 1974 he could have been elected mayor. Vince Scully, the Bronx-born, Manhattan-raised announcer for the Dodgers couldn't help appreciating the irony of the moment:

> "What a marvelous moment for baseball; what a marvelous moment for Atlanta and the state of Georgia; what a marvelous moment for the country and the world. A black man is getting a standing ovation in the Deep South for breaking a record of an all-time baseball idol."

The story of "flight 715" began twenty-seven years prior. Branch Rickey was the president and co-owner of the Brooklyn Dodgers. Rickey, whose family can be traced back to Scotland and Ireland, was born in Stockdale, Ohio, in 1881. He played baseball at Ohio Wesleyan University before playing professionally for a few years. As a ballplayer Rickey was mediocre at best.

Rickey served as an officer in the army during World War I. He fought in France under Gen. John "Black Jack" Pershing. While in France he was in command of a training unit that included baseball greats Ty Cobb, Christy Mathewson, and George Sisler. All three players had interrupted their Major League careers to enlist in the army in 1918.

After the war, Rickey resumed what would be a lifelong career in baseball, but in management. Prior to his arrival in Brooklyn, Rickey had been responsible for introducing many innovations to the game of baseball. While working as president and manager of the St. Louis Cardinals, he developed the Minor League farm system and introduced the batting helmet to protect players from head injuries. He developed a system of statistical analysis, batting cages, and pitching machines.

Rickey was a personal friend of the general manager of the Brooklyn Dodgers, Larry MacPhail. As a baseball executive MacPhail was also innovative. In 1935 he introduced night baseball in Cincinnati by installing lights in Crosley Field and invited President Roosevelt to throw the switch that turned them on. When MacPhail, who had also served in

World War I under General Pershing, was offered an officer's commission in the army in 1942 to serve in World War II, he accepted. Upon MacPhail's departure from the Dodgers, the team offered Rickey the position of general manager. Rickey took the position and continued the trend of making changes.

Rickey's most important innovation came in 1946 when he decided that it was time for baseball at the Major League level to be integrated. At least that was what he said. It is known that Rickey was influenced by the treatment he had seen African Americans endure. For example, during his college baseball days it angered Rickey to see a black teammate treated like a second-class citizen when the team was staying at a hotel for an away game. It is also possible that he was wanted to make the Dodgers the powerhouse of the National League by recruiting from the widest possible selection of good players available. Or perhaps it was his devout Christian (Methodist) faith that compelled him to do the right thing.

There was lots of "talk" during the 1940's about it being time to integrate baseball. Informally integration had begun with off-season exhibition games during the 1930s. There were the "barn-storming" tours of Bob Feller (1962 Hall of Fame inductee), which showcased other Major League stars and Negro League talents such as Satchel Paige. Paige, who pitched for the Kansas City Monarchs in the Negro League, joined up with Jay Hanna "Dizzy" Dean, pitcher for the "gashouse gang" St. Louis Cardinals, and together they sponsored their own country-wide tours during the off season, with Paige's all-black team playing Dean's all-white team. The public interest in interracial games brought tens of thousands of fans to these events.

And the interest continued into the next decade when, in 1946, professional baseball technically had its first integrated game, thanks to the efforts of both Feller and Paige. Feller had worked with Paige in the 1930s, but temporarily left baseball for a tour of duty with the navy on the battleship *USS Alabama*, stationed in the Pacific. Upon his return to the sport in 1946, Feller contacted his friend and the two of them came up with the idea of an actual *series* of games with black players playing against white players. They knew that fan curiosity would result in ticket sales.

However, Branch Rickey was the first person to act on the idea of integrating teams within the Major Leagues. He looked around for the player most suited to the challenge and chose Jackie Robinson. Some people at that time doubted Rickey's motives. Be that as it may, Rickey recruited Robinson from the Negro League team the Kansas City Monarchs and sent him to a Dodger Affiliate team in Montreal. In 1947 Robinson was brought to the majors.

Robinson may not have been the best African American player available at the time, but he possessed the traits Rickey was looking for. Rickey knew that the process of integration would have many obstacles to overcome and would have to be carefully planned. For this reason the Dodgers' manager wanted a ballplayer with courage and intelligence as well as talent. It might have been Robinson's military record that impressed Rickey, who was also a military veteran and who, like President Harry Truman, had served under "Black Jack" Pershing in World War 1 in France. It can be speculated that Rickey was witness to the heroic actions of the "Harlem Hellfighters" during the war. As a veteran he no doubt knew that African Americans also served in World War ll. The general public was also aware that blacks had defended the United States.

Rickey felt that Robinson's college education would work to their advantage. Rickey had thoroughly investigated Robinson's background and was also impressed that Jackie went to church every Sunday. Rickey knew it was going to take an extraordinary man to stand up to the abuse a black player would initially face playing in the majors. He knew that the road to integration in baseball was not going to be smooth walk in the park. He decided that Jackie Robinson was the person for the journey.

Rickey was intending to create across-the-board deseg-regation in baseball. It was not his intention to introduce Robinson into the Major Leagues as a novelty. But he was clever enough to hide his full vision for integration from his colleagues and from the public, at least long enough to implement his plan. At the same time he signed Robinson he was also considering two other African American players, pitcher Don Newcombe and catcher Roy Campanella. Soon after signing Robinson, Rickey did in fact sign Campanella and Newcombe. Like Robinson, these were men of character and vision.

Before bringing Robinson, "Campy," and "Newc" into the majors Rickey knew that they would at need some Minor League experience with white teams. Because of baseball's unwritten law at that time against integration Rickey had to find Minor League managers who wouldn't object to the idea of having a black player assigned to their team. Robinson was sent to the Dodger Minor League team in Montreal. The president of the Montreal Royals, a Dodger affiliate, was Hector Racine. He agreed to Rickey's plan for integration and welcomed Robinson to the team in 1946. He was in agreement with Rickey that integration was necessary. Racine took a lot of heat for his inclusion of black players on the Montreal Royals roster. Many of the Royals' games were cancelled because of Robinson's presence on the team. Hector Racine is a name not usually found in any history of baseball's integration of blacks. But his contribution to the world of sports is of enormous historical importance. He, like Branch Rickey, was committed to the idea of integrating baseball. Racine is quoted as saying "Negroes fought alongside whites and shared the foxhole dangers (in two world wars) and they should get a fair trial in baseball."[19] Like Rickey, Racine was willing to travel the difficult road.

Rickey wasn't merely an idealist. In fact, he was not an idealist at all. He was a man with a plan who was smart enough to anticipate the roadblocks. He knew that assigning all three players to the same team would cause too much resistance from the fans. With this in mind catcher Roy Campanell ("Campy") and pitcher Don Newcombe ("Newc") were sent to a class B club in Nashua, New Hampshire, which was managed by Walter Alston. Rickey and Alston already knew each other from their mutual association with the St. Louis Cardinals when Rickey hired Alston in 1944. Alston played briefly with the Cardinals, but like Rickey was not destined for a Major League playing career. However, Alston would eventually lead the Dodgers to their first World Championship, in 1955, with a team that would include Robinson, Campanella, and Newcombe.

The Nashua team was formed in 1946 specifically for the purpose of creating an entry point for Newcombe and Campanella. Rickey assigned the job of finding the right location for a new minor league team to "Buzzy" Bavasi, who was a business manager in the Dodger organization. Bavasi had just returned from Italy, where he won a Bronze Star as an army machine gunner in the Italian campaign of World War II. He suspected that Rickey was planning to integrate baseball when he got the news that Robinson was signed to a Dodger contract. He was not opposed to the idea. Bavasi, like Rickey, did not allow anything, especially bigotry, to hinder his ability to find and sign the best ballplayers regardless of color. Later Bavasi would become the general manager of the Dodgers. Under his leadership the Dodgers would win eight National League pennants, along with four world championships.

In the meantime, there was much to do to prepare Robinson for the majors, and the majors for Robinson. Rickey talked frankly to his new recruit about the racial situation. They came to an agreement regarding Robinson's response to the inevitable abuse he might experience from the press and the public. With regard to the other players on the Dodgers,

Rickey would not tolerate any complaining about Robinson's presence on the team.

Whatever people may have thought regarding Branch Rickey's motives, he must have had a vision of where baseball needed to go. He knew that he wasn't going to be admired for his plans of integration. He was a shrewd businessman. But he was still willing to risk his financial interest in the Dodger franchise to pursue his vision. He had no way of knowing what the reaction of the Brooklyn fans would be. But he knew that it was a real possibility that the fans would refuse to buy tickets. There was no doubt in his mind that he was going to be criticized by the owners of the other Major League clubs. Under those circumstances it would be safe to say that his motives were exactly what he claimed them to be.

At the same time, the businessman in him refused to let a great opportunity slip by. Rickey knew that the Negro Leagues had enormous talent. He felt that the first major league team to sign the black players was going to get the best players at the best price. He also knew that Mexican brewery czar Jorge Pasquel was raiding the Negro Leagues and signing players to go play in the Mexican League.

Following his good business sense, Rickey set about garnering support for his plans among influential people. Legendary sports announcer Red Barber, who at that time was the Dodger game announcer, said this of Rickey in Ken Burns' documentary *Baseball*:

> "Rickey's determination to desegregate major league
> Baseball was born out of a combination of idealism
> and astute business sense."[20]

When Branch Rickey first told Barber of his plans to hire Jackie Robinson, the announcer, who was a Southerner born in Mississippi, told Rickey he wasn't sure if he could continue announcing the Dodgers' games. However, after meeting Robinson and watching him play, Barber became an ardent supporter of Robinson and later of Campanella and Newcombe. It was becoming apparent that Rickey had chosen the right ballplayers to bring to the majors.

Next, Rickey had to surround Robinson with support from the ball club and its fans. The entire Dodger organization was serious about integration, and this is plain to see by the carefully strategized plan that was put together. For example, before he signed Newcombe and Campanella, Rickey, with the help of Bavasi, found the right city in which to form a Minor League team where they could be placed. He made sure that the team owners and managers were also committed to integration. His plan was carefully laid out to be sure that, in the case of Nashua, New Hampshire, the city had a large French Canadian population. He knew the French Canadians would be more tolerant of integration than the average American. Mimicking Rickey's cleverness, Bavasi appointed Fred Dobens, the publisher of the *Nashua Telegraph*, to be the team president. This was to assure that the team would get support for the integration process from the press.[21]

Another partner in the push for integration was Walter O'Malley, one of the other co-owners of the Dodgers. His association with Rickey's was not a marriage made in heaven. However, he shared Rickey's vision. In 1948 O'Malley instructed Bavasi to find a location for a Dodger spring training facility that would be free from racial incidents now that team had brought all three black players up to the Major Leagues. Bavasi chose Vero Beach, Florida.

The major force in making Rickey's vision a reality was, of course, Robinson, himself, and his trust in his manager. Robinson could have played it safe and stayed where he was, in the Negro League, making good money in the Negro League. But he, like Rickey, had a vision and the courage to see it through. As Marian Anderson had put her faith in Sol Hurok, Robinson trusted Branch Rickey, and Rickey's vision for the world of baseball. The two men had serious conversations about the consequences of their decision, with Rickey offering Robinson good advice on how to handle the situation. This atmosphere of trust between these two men, one black and one white, was absolutely necessary to the success of the venture.

Fortunately Robinson had the talent to go along with his courage and succeeded so well as a ballplayer that the Dodger players and fans were relatively quick to accept his presence on the team (more on this in the second section following this one). In his book *The Boys of Summer,* Roger Kahn writes,

> By applauding Robinson, a fan did not feel that he
> was taking a stand on school integration, or on open
> housing. But for an instant, he had accepted Robin-

son simply as a hometown ballplayer. To disregard color, even for an instant, is to step away from the old prejudices, the old hatred. *That is not a path on which many double back.*

Jackie Robinson's success with the Dodger fans allowed Rickey to bring to Brooklyn the other black players, Campanella and Newcombe, whom he had assigned to the Minor League in New Hampshire. Like Robinson they were exceptional ballplayers and men of strong character.

The Brooklyn fans loved baseball and they loved winning. With Robinson, Newcombe and Campanella, the Dodgers went to the World Series in 1949 to play the New York Yankees. When the first game of the series was played at Yankee Stadium on October 5th the Dodgers put all three of their black players in the starting line-up with Don Newcombe as the starting pitcher. Outside the Stadium there were no protesters, no one picketing, and even the Ku Klux Klan had enough sense not to annoy the 66,224 fans who were attending the game. Ironically, inside the Stadium, the National Anthem was being sung by the official New York Yankee's vocalist, Lucy Monroe. It was ironic because Lucy was a direct descendant of the fifth president of the United States, James Monroe, who himself owned slaves.

For Dodger fans, and all baseball fans, the love of the game was stronger than any human weakness such as prejudice. By 1949 Robinson was so popular and loved that Woodrow Buddy Johnson wrote a song for him, "Did You See Jackie Robinson Hit That Ball?"

No Man Can Hinder Me

There was in the early days of baseball, an official ban against Negro players in professional baseball. It eventually became an unofficial ban, almost like a gentlemen's agreement. In 1945, when Branch Rickey was holding tryouts of black ballplayers, he gave the story that he was putting together a black team. However he was really looking for the right black player to play for the Dodgers. At this time Happy Chandler became the Commissioner of Baseball. He was in favor of integration. Chandler had replaced Kenesaw Mountain Landis, who, as baseball's first commissioner, was strongly opposed to the idea of integrating baseball. When Rickey wanted to sign Robinson, Chandler supported him. Chandler felt he was risking his job by doing this. But at the same time he and Branch Rickey knew it had to be done. And they both knew there was no law against it. There was nothing to hinder them from following their conscience.

In the early 1940's there were several teams considering integration. It has been reported that Bill Veeck wanted to buy the Philadelphia Phillies in 1943 and integrate the team. For Veeck the timing wasn't right. For Rickey, Robinson, and Chandler, however, all the pieces came together. It was almost unnoticed when several months after Rickey signed Robinson, Veeck was finally able to achieve his goal of signing a black player.

Veeck had served three years in the Marines in the South Pacific during World War II. Shortly after his discharge he bought the Cleveland Indians baseball team and signed Lary Doby. Doby played for the Newark (NJ) Eagles of the Negro League and in 1946 led that team to a Negro League World Series Championship. As Veeck had done, Doby had served in the Pacific during World War II, but as a member of the U.S. Navy. As Branch Rickey had done with Jackie Robinson, Veeck placed a lot of emphasis on Doby's character. Veeck knew that Doby would face a lot of abuse as one of the first black major league players. Baseball scouts assured Veeck that Doby was the right person for the challenge.

Under Veeck the Indians became the first American League team to integrate. Veeck, like Rickey, had little tolerance for any of his players who complained about the presence of black teammates.

Many sports historians believe that after the Black Sox Scandal baseball faced a dire future.[22] Baseball fans were losing their love of the game because of the many instances of gambling influencing the outcome of a game. Then along came "The Babe," whom some historians credit as having saved baseball—and, one could argue—leaving a legacy intact for black ballplayers to inherit.

The Babe can also be credited with rebuilding the interest in baseball that reached a peak in the 1940s. In the forties and fifties baseball was not just the "national pastime." It lived in the hearts of most Americans. Ruth had set the stage for Robinson, Doby, Newcombe, and Campanella to have a great impact on life in America. As one team after another integrated, baseball provided white Americans the opportunity to leave their bigotry at the gate when they entered the ballpark. For a couple of hours on a summer afternoon they could enjoy the beauty of life without prejudice. The fans probably didn't notice what was happening to them. But something was happening.

All-Star shortstop Pee Wee Reese played for the Brooklyn Dodgers, and later the Los Angeles Dodgers from 1940 to 1958. He got his name "Pee Wee" when he was a championship marble player ("pee wee" is the name of the small marble). Like many ballplayers, Pee Wee took three years off from his baseball career to join the military during World War II—in his case, the navy. When Pee Wee returned to the Dodgers after the war, Robinson was already with the team. Although a Southerner, Pee-Wee had no strong prejudices regarding blacks. In fact, as captain of the Dodger team, Peewee was a leader in changing the attitudes of some of his teammates who were having trouble accepting Robinson.

Pee Wee also changed the attitude of millions of baseball fans. At a game in Cincinnati in 1947 Robinson was playing second base and Pee Wee was at shortstop. During the pregame warm-up the fans were shouting insults and threats at Robinson. Pee Wee walked over to Jackie, put his arm around him and said something. Whatever Pee Wee said is not known. But the fans were so affected by Pee Wee's action that they immediately went silent.[23]

Pee Wee had a strong positive effect on all of the black ballplayers during the first years of integration. Pitcher Joe

Black of the Dodgers was the first black pitcher to win a World Series game when he beat the Yankees in the opening game in 1952. Black is quoted as saying,

> "Pee Wee helped make my boyhood dream come true to play in the majors, the World Series. When Pee Wee reached out to Jackie, all of us in the Negro League smiled and said it was the first time that a white guy had accepted us. When I finally got up to Brooklyn, I went to Pee Wee and said, 'Black people love you. When you touched Jackie, you touched all of us.' With Pee Wee, it was No. 1 on his uniform and No. 1 in our hearts."[24]

Robinson and Rickey gave the ballplayers the opportunity to get to know one another in an environment that called for mutual success. The white ballplayers got to witness Robinson's ability as an athlete. They also got to witness his character. Bobby Bragan, one of the players on the 1948 Dodger team said that knowing Jackie changed his opinion about "coloreds."

As team after team integrated in the 1950s baseball fans were taking the presence of black players as the norm. Yankee fans were actually getting impatient before the arrival of Elston Howard, the first African American to join the "Bronx Bombers." Howard was finally signed by the Yankees in 1955. His journey to the majors was delayed for two years as he fulfilled his military obligation. When Willie Mays joined the Giants in 1951, the younger fans thought nothing of the fact that he was black. (Like Elston Howard and Don Newcomb, Mays also missed a few years while he was serving his two-year military obligation.) By 1955 New

York Yankee fans were not just willing to tolerate integration, they were demanding it.

In the meantime, Happy Chandler did lose his job as Commissioner of Baseball as a result of his support of Branch Rickey. Rickey, however, continued in baseball. He continued pursuing his goal of integrating baseball when he left the Dodger organization in the early 1950s and became general manager of the Pittsburg Pirates. In 1954 Rickey again broke the color line by signing Curt Roberts, and one year later Roberto Clemente, to play for this team. Roberto Clementi had actually played in the Dodger minor league system. He was being groomed to play for the Dodgers. When Rickey left the Dodger organization he managed to bring the future Hall of Fame outfielder, Clementi, over to Pittsburgh.

By 1959 when the Boston Red Sox signed Pumpsie Green, the world of baseball had successfully eliminated segregation from the base-paths and created an even playing field for black athletes. The whole process of integration took eight years to be 99 percent complete, with all teams but one (the Red Sox) having recruited at least one black player by the year 1955. And it took only twelve years for the stubborn owners of the Boston team to realize that integration was better than segregation. There were still some issues involving hotels and restaurants refusing to serve blacks, including African American ballplayers traveling with their teams, but even that situation was resolved within a few years.

As baseball teams became integrated, black ballplayers were also changing. They were beginning to lose their suspicion of whites. No one spoke of it, at least in public, but the black players were beginning to appreciate the fans appreciation of them. They began to think of themselves not as a novelty, but as an integral part of the game and an integral part of American culture. Friendships on the teams were forming across racial lines.

The game of baseball provided a real-life opportunity to work out one of life's major problems. The ballpark was the laboratory where integration was tested–and found to work quite well. As the baby boomers became old enough to go to a ballgame they got their first immunization against prejudice. By 1955, the first wave of "boomers" were celebrating their tenth birthday. Many of them were treasuring their baseball cards with pictures of their favorite players, and arguing with each other as to who was the better catcher, Yogi Berra, the Italian American catcher for the Yankees or Roy Campanella, the African American catcher for the Dodgers. The argument was based on anything and everything, but not race.

The game of baseball was the national pastime for blacks and whites alike. By 1955 no matter what Major League game was being played, there was going to be an African American on the field. By 1955 three out of four families had a television. No longer just a form of entertainment, television was a "way of life," and a way of seeing life. Just as white parents and children were glued to the TV watching a baseball game, blacks were equally captivated. Henry Lewis Gates, a renowned African American professor at Harvard University, in his book, *Colored People*, recalls how his father and older brother were bonded by their mutual love of the game of baseball and their team, the Pittsburgh Pirates. Throughout the country blacks and whites, young and old, were watching the same games and the same players at the same time. Inning by inning the separation of races was becoming something most people didn't want. And unbeknownst to all, they were forming a bond that ultimately resulted in a total desegregation of baseball as well as other major professional and collegiate sports such as basketball and football. Furthermore, this social movement, which was channeled through the world of sports, also opened the doors and paved the way for athletes from other nations and cultures such as Japan, Korea, China, Eastern and Western European countries, and Latin America.

The nay-sayers who protested that blacks were taking jobs away from white athletes turned out to be totally wrong. In 1957 the Brooklyn Dodgers moved the franchise to Los Angeles. The Dodgers were soon followed by the New York (baseball) Giants who relocated to San Francisco. As Major League baseball expanded west of the Mississippi and nine teams were added to the leagues, the new complaint was that the pool of talent was not keeping up with the expansion.

It is impossible to mention every person and event in sports that contributed to the destruction of segregation. Several persons and teams, however, deserve special mention. One person, for example, who cannot be left out is the black boxer Joe Louis, the heavyweight champion from 1937 until 1949.

His cultural impact was felt well outside the ring. Lewis is widely regarded as the first African American to achieve the status of a nationwide hero within the United

States, and was also a focal point of anti-Nazi sentiment leading up to and during World War II. He also was instrumental in integrating the game of golf, breaking the sport's color barrier in America by appearing under a sponsor's exemption in a PGA event in 1952.

Congress stated that he "did so much to bolster the spirit of the American people during one of the most crucial times in American history which has endured throughout the years as a symbol of strength for the nation." Following Louis's death, President Ronald Reagan said, "Joe Louis was more than a sports legend—his career was an indictment of racial bigotry and a source of pride and inspiration to millions of white and black people around the world."

It is also necessary to mention the most unique sports team of all time, The Harlem Globetrotters. The Globetrotters came to national attention around 1929 under the business direction of a manager who inhabited the other end of the height spectrum: the five-foot five-inch London born Polish Jew, Abe Saperstein. Abe had a vision of the impact black players were going to have on the game of basketball. The Globetrotters was a specialized basketball team that played only exhibition games. Their specialty was comedy. Their antics on the court disguised their true athletic ability, and attracted more fans than the professional white teams playing serious basketball.

In 1948 professional basketball was separated by race. There were black teams and there were white teams. But sports fans wanted to see a black versus white game. People were more than a little curious about the Globetrotters' ability to play serious basketball. So, in 1948 the Globetrotters challenged the champion Minneapolis Lakers to a game. There was no problem selling thousands of tickets. On a last-second set shot the Globetrotters won. The fans' curiosity was satisfied and that of the owners of the white teams was piqued. The Lakers and the Globetrotters continued to play each other for several years in exhibition games.

It would be impossible to measure the effect that the Globetrotters had on the attitude of white Americans, but there can be no doubt that the effect was positive. Their use of comedy was an extraordinarily effective means of diluting prejudice and simultaneously creating a venue that allowed the public, black and white, to witness their disguised but nevertheless recognized skill at playing the game.

And there can be no doubt that one of the first black players to sign a contract to play in the National Basketball Association, Nat "Sweetwater Clifton," came from the Globe-trotters. Like other pioneers of integration around this time, Clifton was also a World War II veteran. In 1950 the New York Knickerbockers selected him in the first round of the draft and signed him. Clifton was very comfortable playing against white ballplayers. During his three-year service in the army, 1944–47, he was usually playing on integrated teams.

While it was true that before 1950 blacks were exclud-ed from the league that would eventually become the Na-tional Basketball Association, the style of basketball played by Abe Saperstein's Globetrotters was of enormous impor-tance in popularizing the game in an industry that would be of enormous importance to blacks. Although Abe Saperstein was known to have shortchanged some of his players regarding salaries, he created a situation that enabled many of his players to go on to successful careers in the post-1950 integrated NBA.

It was not a totally smooth evolution from segregation to integration during the 1950s in the world of professional basketball. But it took less than one generation from the day that the NBA drafted its first black player until the day that the NBA had its first black head coach.

The Boston Celtics' head coach in 1950 was Red Auerbach, a Russian Jewish immigrant. The first black player to be drafted by the National Basketball Association was selected by Auerbach, The player was Chuck Cooper,[25] a graduate of Duquesne University, a Catholic school in Pittsburgh. Auerbach chose Cooper over future Hall of Famer Bob Cousy.

During the early 1950s the black players were not a 100 percent welcome by the white players.[26] By 1960, however, the contribution that the black players were making to the game of basketball, and the other major team sports, made racial prejudice an unpopular attitude among the players and the fans. By 1960 two of the top three college basketball players drafted were African Americans. At the same time it was apparent to the unbiased observer that the road to a head coaching position for a black player was under construction. And by 1966 Bill Russell, an African American who played the post position for Boston Celtics, was given one of the most envied positions in basketball—head coach of his alma mater, which happened to be basketball's premier team. From start to finish the whole process of integration in basketball took less than one generation.

The game of basketball was so exciting that the desire to see the ball go through the hoop blocked out any concern about the color of the player. The desire to win at all costs afforded the elimination of segregation. And the cost was actually very low. During the 1950s integration in basketball, as in baseball, was creating scenes of an integrated American lifestyle that made integration appear perfectly normal. In less than one generation college and professional basketball were virtually completely integrated. The large numbers of baby boomers entering college in the mid-1960s were educated in an environment that had only traces of segregation.

In the world of sports in the late 1950s, the arguments about the possibility of black athletes becoming managers, coaches, or even professional football quarterbacks were based on perceptions of the athletes' potential as managers, coaches, or quarterbacks. It was common perception that black athletes did not possess certain qualities necessary for these positions. By 1960 the discussions were no longer about the rights of a black athlete. The discussions were about qualifications. The black athletes of that time, through their talent and character, quickly revealed the "common perception" to be a "misconception."

In 1960 America was becoming a country where a person's ability and character were more important than the color of his or her skin.

Without making any laws or breaking any laws, Branch Rickey and Jackie Robinson made the American dream more accessible to everyone. Another section of the wall of prejudice, one that looked as unreachable as the center field wall at the Polo Grounds, came down.[27] Working as a team, Rickey and Robinson, as well as Veeck and Doby, accomplished what couldn't be accomplished by any number of people working from just one side of the wall of segregation. But with someone on one side pushing and someone else on the other side pulling, the wall just fell.

The genius of Branch Rickey is that he knew, like a skilled military general, where he could win the battle. He didn't frustrate himself by going to Washington to get a law passed against segregation in baseball. There was no law on the books requiring segregation. He didn't call a press conference. In fact he disguised his plans. He chose his battle carefully. And he knew that no one could stop him, or to paraphrase the black spiritual "No One Could Hinder Him." The genius of athletes like Jackie Robinson and Bill Russell was their ability to see the future and demonstrate the patience to allow it to unfold properly.

Without making any laws or breaking any laws, without accusation or anger, professional athletes created a world in which prejudice was doomed. It was a world that tens of millions of young and old Americans wanted to be a part of, even if only vicariously. And to be a part of it you couldn't exclude African Americans.

Branch Rickey's dream of integrating the world of sports took only about fifteen years to complete when African American football player, Bobby Mitchell, took the field as a Washington Redskin.[28] Jackie Robinson's dream of seeing an African American as manager of a major league baseball team took a little longer. But the inevitable happened when Frank Robinson assumed the helm of the Cleveland Indians in 1975.

Sports in general, and most importantly baseball, were an antidote and a vaccine for prejudice. For many older white sports fans their opinions about African Americans were modified and often reversed by what they saw on the playing field. For older blacks their skepticism and mistrust of whites was mitigated. For the younger fans, black and white, many of them never acquired the disease of prejudice—or at least not to the same extent as did previous generations—because so many of their heroes on the playing field were people of another color.

Chapter 7
"Onward Christian Soldiers"

Steps toward a Racially Integrated Military in World War II

In the stories behind the athletes and managers who made integration possible in professional sports, there is one biographical detail that comes up again and again: black or white, many of these men had served in the military. It might be significant to mention, for example, that when Jackie Robinson joined the Dodgers, about half of the team's roster, were, like Robinson, World War II veterans.

At this point in time it would be difficult to prove, but one could speculate that they felt something of a bond with a fellow veteran. Sociologists have long noticed this phenomenon. Military sociologist Charles Moskos has gone so far as to advocate restoring the military draft, insisting that a shared military experience for Americans of different classes, races, and economic backgrounds forges a sense of common purpose.[29]

Throughout the twentieth century the military evolved into a powerful agent for social change, realizing the vision of at least one very influential leader—General John

Pershing. His belief in the ability of black soldiers has already been discussed in chapter 3, along with their remarkable accomplishments under his command in the Spanish American War and World War I. From his beginnings as a teacher in a black school in Missouri, to his prominence in the military, Pershing worked with and inspired any number of Americans who would become influential leaders in their own right—starting with Teddy Roosevelt.

It was in the Battle of San Juan Hill during the Spanish-American War where Pershing and his black troops fought alongside future president, then-Lieutenant Theodore Roosevelt of the Rough Riders. Roosevelt was no doubt impressed by Pershing's men, who accompanied him on his historic charge up the hill. He was quoted as writing to a friend, "I wish no better men beside me in battle than these colored troops showed themselves to be." Roosevelt's growing awareness that African Americans share the same potential as white soldiers would be felt by other political leaders, such as Presidents Truman and Eisenhower, as well as by General George Patton and others who had also served with Pershing in the military.

Roosevelt's perspectives on race were more complicated than the usual sentiment of his era. His father, Theodore Roosevelt, was a northerner who had supported Abraham Lincoln and the Union effort during the Civil War. His mother, Martha Bullock, was a southern belle from a Georgia slave-owning family. She maintained her Confederate sympathies. No doubt this unlikely marriage offered a young Roosevelt the opportunity to comprehend both points of view. But he eventually came to the conclusion that the best thing for America would be an attitude of non-prejudice.

As William McKinley's vice-president, elected in 1900 for McKinley's second term, Roosevelt shared the president's view that the success of the nation depended on racial equality. McKinley had expressed this opinion in several speeches he made, and even in a visit to the famous Tuskegee Institute, during his presidency. Roosevelt became president after McKinley's assassination in 1901, and continued the push for better race relations, at least through his actions if not so much through words.

In a famous statement that has raised some controversy, Roosevelt said, "I have not been able to think out any solution of the terrible problem offered by the presence of the Negro on this continent, but of one thing I am sure, and that is that inasmuch as he is here and can neither be killed nor driven away, the only wise and honorable and Christian thing to do is to treat each black man and each white man strictly on his merits as a man, giving him no more and no less that he shows himself worthy to have."[30] Although by today's standards such words might not sound magnanimous, they pointed the way to a more rational if not heartfelt way of viewing race relations.

As hard as it may be to understand, the president, whether it was McKinley or Roosevelt, could not change people's feeling about race by pushing laws through Congress, especially during those years. There, however, other measures that could be taken to pave the way.

Gregory Salvatore Scime

Roosevelt, in his determination to defeat racial prejudice, found an effective expression in a non-legislative action. Upon becoming president, Roosevelt created a national controversy when, on October 1st, 1901, he invited Booker T. Washington to dinner at the Whitehouse. Booker Washington may have aroused mixed feelings among blacks but was among the most revered spokespersons of African Americans at the time. Roosevelt was known to have some negative bias toward the general intelligence of African Americans. But he had no bias about their right to equal status in the United States. Roosevelt wanted to discuss with Washington issues relating to Southern blacks.[31]

The reaction to this invitation made national headlines. Southerners were appalled that a black person would be sitting at the dinner table with Roosevelt's wife. Even some Northerners were displeased. But it sent a message to the African American community that a black man could walk through the front door of the White House and have dinner with the president.[32]

It is not possible that President Roosevelt was unaware of the total impact of this dinner invitation, given the political and social climate at that time. He no doubt anticipated the public reaction. After all, he was a politician. He was also a military man. He no doubt calculated the potential losses, weighed them against the gains, and decided to act upon his belief that racial equality was necessary for the future success of the country. President Roosevelt also knew that he did not need the approval of Congress, or the Supreme Court, or the making or breaking of any laws to extend a dinner invitation. And he knew that no one could stop him.

There should be no doubt that the historic dinner at the White House softened the attitudes of many whites at the time. As recently as 2008, then-presidential candidate Sen. John McCain referred to the dinner invitation in his concession speech when Barack Obama was elected, noting that the 20th century began with a White House dinner invitation to an African American, and ended with an African American in a position to extend White House dinner invitations.[33]

Theodore Roosevelt was one of many leaders to be inspired by General Pershing in the push toward racial equality.

When the United States entered World War I Pershing petitioned the army to allow him to use African American soldiers for combat duties. The army rejected the request. But, as explained in chapter 3, Pershing found a way to get the 369th Harlem Hellfighters to the front line in France, which set the stage for a very important collaboration.

Major Harry Truman, who, in 1945 would become the country's thirty-third president, had served in the American Expeditionary Force commanded by General Pershing in France during World War I. It was during his time in

Gregory Salvatore Scime

France that Truman witnessed the valor and talent of the 369th Harlem Hellfighters.

Like presidents before and after, Truman must have taken his oath of office seriously when he promised to uphold the Constitution, especially the part about all men being equal. As a senator from Missouri he had already helped put through legislation in 1940 that eventually led to the training of Negro pilots in the Army Air Corps. As president, Truman issued Executive Order 9980, which required civil service jobs to be offered on a nondiscriminatory basis. He went a step further in 1948, on July 26, just eleven days after General Pershing's death, when he issued Executive Order 9981, which states the following:

"It is hereby declared to be the policy of the President that there shall be equality of treatment and opportunity for all persons in the armed services without regard to race, color, religion, or national origin."

The order also established the President's Committee on Equality of Treatment and Opportunity in the Armed Forces.

Prior to Executive Order 9981 President Truman had tried to eliminate segregation in the armed forces by having Congress pass a law against it. But in 1948 Congress voted down all attempts by the president to end discrimination. When Truman issued executive order 9981, however, he was acting as Commander in Chief of the Armed Forces. It was not his position as President but his position as Commander in Chief that gave him the unilateral authority to make

78

policies regarding the military. In this capacity he was not required by the Constitution to consult Congress on most matters involving the military. Keeping his constitutional rights in mind, Truman simply did what he knew was right without needing the vote of Congress.

When Truman desegregated the armed forces he effectively desegregated all of the schools on military bases. Six years before the Supreme Court decision *Brown v. The Board of Education*, dependent children of active duty military personnel were attending integrated schools. Even prior to Executive Order 9981, the War Department in 1943 ordered the desegregation of all military recreation facilities. In 1944 it ordered the desegregation of military buses.[34] And there was never a separate pay scale for African Americans. All military personnel were paid according to rank and time in service. The desegregation of the armed forces also implicitly called for desegregation of military housing, military hospitals, and mess halls.

Truman's presidency was followed by that of Dwight D. Eisenhower, who was also among a generation of generals who regarded John Pershing as a mentor. As General in World War II, Eisenhower allowed integrated combat units in the European Theater; as president during the 1950s, he eliminated the last remnants of segregated schools on military bases. The armed forces had proven that integration could be accomplished without riots, civil disobedience, or even coverage by the news media.

If the armed forces could produce political leaders willing and able to battle discrimination, it was because the military served as a type of social laboratory where necessity forced cooperation and where ability would be recognized and put to use.

During World War II African American soldiers, sailors, marines, and aviators were performing combat duties only in segregated units. There were exceptions. In the war in the Pacific all personnel on naval ships, including African Americans, had battle stations assigned without regard to color. The Coast Guard also had integrated battle stations. And, as just mentioned, the army would integrate its combat units in the European Theater during World War II.

But the journey toward integration throughout the armed forces did not start smoothly. At the outbreak of World War II, attitudes were mixed as to whether "colored" soldiers should be used in combat, let alone serve side by side with their white counterparts. This was particularly true in the Army and Army Air Corp. On the positive side, Gen. Lesley J. McNair, Commander of Army Ground Forces in 1941, argued that African American units *should* be used in combat. On the other hand, Gen. Omar Bradley, at the time Army Chief of Staff, referred to integration in the military as an ill-advised "social experiment" that needed to be tried in the civilian world first.

Whatever the mix of opinions, in the end it was the need for military manpower that would ultimately trump racial attitudes during World War II. And before the issue of integration could be grappled with, many individuals in the military and the public first needed to see that African Americans were fit to fight. The Tuskegee Airmen were perhaps the most famous African Americans to provide such proof.

At the onset of World War II it was the opinion of many military leaders that blacks could not be trained to fly. African Americans wanting to serve their country in the air corps, however, pressured the army to accommodate them. In 1941, under President Franklin Roosevelt's administration, Kentucky-born U.S. Army Air Corp officer Noel Parrish was delegated to find a suitable location to create a flight school where potential African American pilots would be trained. The son of a minister, Parrish was known to have an insatiable curiosity and interest in people of all colors. He was an efficient and careful leader. He began his assignment by gathering as much information as he could find regarding the "American Negro." Demonstrating a thorough, methodological approach characteristic of his military background, Parrish read books and interviewed anthropologists, politicians, and black newspaper editors. He concluded what his potential students already knew: Negroes can fly a plane. The location he selected for the training school was Tuskegee, Alabama, partly because a black civilian flight training facility already existed there.

The army next faced a short but heated debate in Congress, in which it had to face down opposition from Southern Democrats, who viewed combat-ready African American pilots as a threat to segregation policies. On the flip side,

Gregory Salvatore Scime

the army also received criticism from civil rights leaders on the grounds that the all-black training facility itself was a step backward *toward* segregation. Fortunately the Army Air Corp commanders knew better than to take advice from politicians or even from civil rights leaders and they proceeded with their plan to train Negro pilots. Despite the challenges, in less than one year the flight school in Tuskegee was ready to accept black Air Corp trainees.

The group of men who trained there came to be known as the Tuskegee Airmen. By 1943, at the height of World War II, black pilots of the Tuskegee school were flying combat missions in the European theater. One of these pilots was Wendell O. Pruitt, who is credited with singlehandedly sinking an enemy ship in addition to destroying many enemy aircraft in "dogfights." By 1944 the Tuskegee Airmen were escorting heavy bombers in raids over Europe, protecting them from enemy aircraft. Their flying skill had become legendary.

In the short span of six years, the U.S. Air Force (which was formerly the Army Air Corp) out of necessity came to the conclusion in 1947, one year before the actual integration of the military, that integration had to be implemented. There was a manpower shortage in the all-white squadrons that could be easily filled with black aviators from the 99th Pursuit Squadron, the Tuskegee Airmen. "Easily filled" because the black airmen were qualified; qualified not only as aviators, but as "officers and gentlemen."

The black pilots of Tuskegee were men of vision. They realized that their contribution to the war was going to preserve the freedom of the United States and that freedom would eventually be available to all Negros in America. These pilots were men who had the courage to pursue that vision, even though they knew that they might not survive the perils of war to experience the freedom they were fighting for.

The battle on the European continent after the D-Day invasion of 1944 met with similar shortages that were remedied with black military talent. When General George S. Patton, known for his expertise in tank warfare, needed more tanks for the march through France in 1944, he called for the 761st Tank Battalion, which was an all-black unit. He did not choose these men because they were black. He chose them because they were qualified.

The 761st Tank Battalion was formed in April of 1942 at Camp Claiborne, Louisiana. It was made up of African American soldiers and commanded by Col. Paul Bates, who was white. (Jackie Robinson, who later became the first black major league baseball player, was originally assigned to the 761st.) The battalion trained for two years, finishing up at Fort Hood, Texas. It was considered for deployment in Europe because it had been given a superior rating by General Ben Lear.[35]

When the 761st Battalion landed on Omaha Beach in France in October of 1944, it was put under the command of Gen. George S. Patton. Patton initially had doubts about their combat readiness. He changed his opinion when he saw the black tankers in action. In a pre-battle speech delivered at St. Nicholas, France, on November 2, 1944, Patton said this to his African American troops:

> "Men, you're the first Negro tankers to ever fight in the American Army. I would never have asked for you if you weren't good. I have nothing but the best in my Army. I don't care what color you are … . Everyone has their eyes on you and is expecting great things from you. Most of all, your race is looking forward to you. Don't let them down, and *damn you, don't let me down!*"

The use of the Black Panther Tankers was a double-edged sword. One side cut through the racial prejudice that white soldiers may have had, while the other side convinced black soldiers that in the final analysis the army doesn't care about the color of anyone's skin.

With the triumphs of all-black fighting units came a gradual shift toward actual integration. Later in that same year, 1944, by order of General Eisenhower, black soldiers fought alongside white troops in the Battle of the Bulge. This is commonly viewed as the first time black and white soldiers fought side by side. Eisenhower was criticized for his use of black troops, especially by his own army chief of staff, Lieutenant. General Walter Bedell Smith.[36] Eisenhower paid no attention to the criticism because he had a shortage of manpower that could be solved only by integration. Eisenhower wasn't trying to start a civil rights movement, or get Congress to pass legislation; he was interested only in winning the war.

As noted earlier in this chapter, naval ships in the Pacific were one of the few exceptions where integration had already taken place by the beginning of the war. Nevertheless, the implementation of the policy required a push from people in both high and low places. Some naval leaders in the early 1940s, including the Secretary of the Navy, Frank Knox, believed that integration could not work because segregation was a national pattern. With a little bit of prompting by President Franklin Roosevelt, it didn't take Knox long to reconsider this position, drawing, as he probably did, upon lessons learned when he had served under General Pershing in World War I. In the meantime, President Roosevelt appointed James Forrestal as Under-Secretary of the Navy. The son of Irish immigrants and a devout Catholic, Forrestal was keen on seeing integration come about. His concern, combined with the efforts of vocal integration advocate Chris Sargent (a white junior office and son of an Episcopalian minister), pressured the navy to begin experimenting with integration aboard combat vessels. The experiment was not to determine *if* integration could work. Forrestal and Sargent were already convinced of this. The experiment was to figure out *how* to make it work—and it obviously succeeded.

Throughout the remainder of the war years the navy was slowly incorporating African Americans into the overall fabric of naval combat readiness. Resistance among white sailors quickly dissipated as their experience with black sailors under combat conditions gave them the opportunity to trust their brothers in arms.

The navy was eventually joined in these efforts by the army—as previously noted in the discussion of General Eisenhower at the Battle of the Bulge. After World War II ended in 1945, integration became competitive. Each branch of the service wanted to outdo the other. Competition among the branches of the armed forces became a source energy propelling integration.

As early as 1941 there actually had been a growing sense among some of the highest commanders across the branches of the armed forces that integration might be necessary. The military commissioned studies regarding the matter. The reports showed segregation to be a problem in that it was preventing the armed forces from operating at their maximum efficiency, placing on them a heavy burden of manpower shortages. But before implementing integration, the researchers, who were themselves military personnel, identified the problems that existed in the segregated units and created a plan of integration that addressed these challenges.

An important point to bear in mind is that the armed forces were not considering the moral aspects of segregation. They were focused on the practical aspects. They knew that in combat situations the stakes were life and death; the plan had to be thought out and it had to work the first time. Those in positions to implement the change took their time because they had to get it right. There was no precedent to guide them. There was no "how to" book on integration.

Nonetheless there was a guiding principle for those who were willing to put their life on the line to protect America. They needed to trust everyone else who was on that line. They knew that everyone in combat, whether in a front line unit or a support unit, had to have a sense of brotherhood that was not hindered by a color line.

The level of racial integration achieved by the military in the 1940's could not be as efficiently achieved in civilian society at large. Nevertheless, the inroads made by the military into the problem of race relations would have some positive ramifications for black veterans re-entering civilian life.

The American military is an intriguing culture. Things that could never be done quickly in the civilian world are easily accomplished in the military world. If someone with a bar or a star on his shoulder wants something to happen, it happens. And sometimes this influence trickles into the civilian world. Such was the case when in 1943 the army commissioned the great American songwriter Irving Berlin[37] to create a Broadway-style musical for the purpose of boosting morale and at the same time raising money for the Army Relief Fund. "This Is the Army" was the title Berlin gave to his show.[38] The cast included active-duty soldiers, black and white, who were actors in civilian life. Berlin insisted that the soldiers live together and perform together on stage. Broadway had never witnessed integration on the performing stage before, and Berlin, who, as a Russian Jewish immigrant had experienced firsthand the terrors of prejudice in his native country, must have realized that his decision might not be popular.

Berlin, however, was one of the most important Broadway composers in 1943. He is credited with having written music for eighteen Broadway shows and nineteen Hollywood movies. No one was going to tell him what he could or couldn't do on stage. As far as the army was concerned, if someone of high enough rank says the black and white soldiers will live and appear on stage together, you can consider it done. Here was a situation where the armed forces joined forces with the musical world to overcome racial barriers that had been in place for generations.

Certainly not all efforts at integration worked out as smoothly in the civilian world—as witnessed in Truman's struggle in Congress to enforce integration—but promising outcomes occasionally did surface for African American veterans.

One such outcome was the Servicemen's Readjustment Act of 1944, which is commonly referred to as the G.I. Bill. It provided benefits to veterans coming home from the war, benefits that included money for education, stipends while going to school, secured loans for home ownership, and medical benefits to veterans and their dependents. Even before World War II blacks placed great emphasis on education. The G.I. Bill made the goal of education, especially a college education, available to every veteran. The bill also created de facto integration at many colleges, because now tens of thousands of African American veterans were going to school. Although integration began slowly, it took less than one generation for colleges all over America to implement a nonbiased admissions process. It is well documented that higher education creates racial tolerance, in both directions.

There were, however, many shortcomings in the disbursement of benefits based on race. These flaws came about not because the G.I. Bill was designed to discriminate. They were due more to conditions outside the military. But the effect of the bill on promoting higher education among black veterans was very significant. The number of African Americans who enrolled in college after the war more than doubled when compared to previous years. Moreover, in great numbers veterans, black and white, with money from the G.I. Bill, were enrolling in trade schools and learning skills that were necessary for the economic boom that followed the war. The rate of home ownership among African Americans increased. Despite the shortcomings, the G.I. Bill provided a road for both black and white veterans to work their way into the middle class. Moreover the G.I. bill helped create a middle-class economy for the returning veterans to enter.

With the enactment of Executive Order 9981 in 1948, officially integrating all of the armed forces, African Americans could begin to sense that their contributions were being taken seriously by the chain of command, right up to the Commander in Chief, the President. Black military men had already demonstrated their patriotism and civic responsibility when they chose to enlist in large numbers each time America was called upon to defend liberties. Now there was evidence of the wisdom behind their decision.

African Americans who served in the armed forces, even before 1948, received equal pay, ate the same food, wore the same clothes as did their white counterparts. African Americans who served after 1948 experienced in the armed forces a life-style that was free from most of the inequalities of civilian life.

Because of the manner in which it was carried out, the integration of the armed forces was accomplished with few glitches.

In March of 1951 the Army asked Johns Hopkins University's operations research office to analyze the impact that integration had on its forces. Extensive surveys of troops and analysis of combat performance in Korea revealed the following:

- Integration raised the morale of African American soldiers and did not reduce that of white soldiers
- Integration was favored by black soldiers and was not opposed by most white soldiers
- Experience in integrated units increased white support for integration
- Integration improved fighting effectiveness[39]

However, even prior to the Korean conflict, opinion surveys were taken among white soldiers serving in integrated unit. The vast majority of white servicemen said they were comfortable serving with black servicemen.

There are many reasons for the success of integration in the armed forces.

Among the reasons is the general overall integrity of the men and women who serve their country. Another reason, simply stated, is that the armed forces anticipate problems and work out solutions before taking action. Years before the issuance of Executive Order 9981, the War Department was in fact preparing for integration. The President Harry Truman Library contains many letters from high-ranking officials of the armed forces arguing the case for desegregation.

The armed forces have also been successful in integrating women, as well as gays and lesbians, into military life without major incident. The integration was accomplished with careful and patient planning.

Without making any laws or breaking any laws (executive orders are directives, not laws) the United States Armed Forces, within a few years, became totally integrated and non-discriminatory. The African American soldiers who fought in the Revolutionary War, Spanish American War, and the two World Wars did more than help to defeat America's enemies abroad. As the abolitionists hoped for in the Civil War, they defeated the enemy at home that would have eventually destroyed the country: racial discrimination. They defeated it not with guns or bombs, but with valor, courage, honor, patriotism.

Chapter 8
"Rock a My Soul"

Little Rock and Rock & Roll Educate TV Audiences
of the 1950s

Looked at separately no one could have seen the road that was being built into the heart and soul of America. After all, of what political importance is jazz? And baseball? It's just a game. The army? Who cares?

By the 1950s these popular institutions were changing the way Americans tolerated discrimination. White Americans were beginning to feel the benefits of giving up prejudice. Each new generation that was born was coming into a world that allowed them to experience life with fewer and fewer walls of separation. Each time a section of the wall came down the rest of the wall got weaker. Americans, black and white, who were born during the baby boom took it for granted that jazz, baseball, and the armed forces were integrated. Further integration was becoming less and less difficult. The races were beginning to trust each other. Racial prejudice still existed, but it was becoming less and less a pattern of American life.

One tool that proved vastly effective in bringing the races together during the 1950s was television, the medium through which increasing numbers of Americans were beginning to experience entertainment, sports, and news.

Television was relatively new, but by the middle of the decade almost every house and apartment had one. Through television, one of the most dramatic moments in the history of American race relations would be seen by an entire nation—black children attending their first day at a previously all-white school in Little Rock, Arkansas.

On September 4, 1957, Americans saw the events in Little Rock on the nightly news. They got to see the rabid anger of the residents of Little Rock as they tried to prevent a few young black girls from entering a school. It was not a pretty sight. However, black Americans saw the U.S. Armed Forces protecting the children. It must have been a bit confusing. White Americans saw the type of irrational anger that prejudice can create. These scenes might not have changed the minds of many white adults at the time, but they gave young viewers of all races the opportunity to see the ugliness of prejudice and the beauty of the Constitution at an impressionable age. These broadcasts formed a pivotal moment in the conscience of a new generation of Americans.

This new generation was the baby boomers, who as adults would do much to close the gap between blacks and whites in America. The man who sent in the armed forces, thereby upholding the Supreme Court's ruling that segregation in schools was illegal, was a military man from an older generation: President Dwight Eisenhower.[40] Eisenhower was acting as Commander in Chief of the Armed Forces when he ordered the National Guard to protect the civil rights of those students.

In contrast to Little Rock, where the law had to be upheld through physical force, the world of popular music had been integrating much more smoothly throughout the 1950s. While whites in Arkansas were listening to radio station KAAY play the Delta Blues of black musicians like Sonny Boy Williamson and Pinetop Perkins, whites in places like New York were listening to the sounds of 1010 WINS Radio (WNJR) as Alan Freed was introducing the Rhythm & Blues of black performers like Fats Domino, Little Richard, and Big Joe Turner. Both styles of blues were inspiring white performers like Elvis Presley, Bill Haley, and others to create the disguised version of R&B that was to be called rock & roll.

Through the 1930s and 1940s two African American vocal groups, the Ink Spots and the Mills Brothers, had been creating a distinctive style of music characterized by a lead singer and three "backup" singers harmonizing. The most popular songs recorded by the Ink Spots were "If I Didn't Care" and "My Prayer." The Mills Brothers had hit songs with "Up a Lazy River" and "Paper Doll." The style was quickly adopted by black vocal groups called Gospel Quartets. Among the most famous of these quartets were the Swan Silvertones, the Golden Gate Quartet, and the Soul Stirrers.. The style of the gospel quartets was the same as the vocal style of the Inkspots and Mills Brothers. However, the gospel groups used religious lyrics instead of secular lyrics. In the 1950s white vocal groups created their own version of Gospel Quartet with lyrics about love and life as seen by a typical teenager of the era. The music world called it "Doo-Wop" because of the nonsensical syllables used by the backup singers. Though the style was completely different than R&B, Doo-Wop was also given the label "rock & roll."

For a while the scene in "rock & roll" was similar to jazz twenty years prior. Black musicians were performing to white segregated audiences; white musicians were copying the style of the black musicians and performing to segregated audiences. There was a line in the sand separating the black musicians from the white musicians. But this separation had all of the permanence of a line in the sand. It lasted about as long it takes for the tide to come in and wash it away.

Four black members of the U.S. Air Force stationed in Pittsburgh formed a vocal group in 1955. When they lost two of the singers to transfers, they "drafted" another airman, baritone David Lerchey, into the group. Lerchey happened to be white, but to the men in blue the distinction between black and white had been demoted seven years ago when the armed forces were integrated. Integration was not what they were pursuing when they invited Lerchey to join the group. They just wanted to sing. The group called themselves the Del-Vikings. When their second hit song, "Come Go with Me," propelled itself into the Billboard Top 10 in 1957, the group had introduced integration into the world of rock & roll. The teenage audiences for this music were also integrating to the beat of Chuck Berry's "Johnny B. Good."

Throughout the 1950s, integration, energized by rock & roll and other kinds of music, was quietly happening throughout the country and in a variety of media. As with national news events like those at Little Rock, television added a sense of immediacy to the world of entertainment—but in the case of these broadcasts there was also a strong sense of community in which blacks and whites could interact.

In a move that must have been aimed at American music lovers of all ages, the executives at NBC decided in the mid-1950s that Nat King Cole should have his own show. He was an African American singer and jazz pianist who enjoyed tremendous popularity by this time. Among his hits was the song "Unforgettable." NBC and Nat King Cole knew that the show was not going to make money because in 1956 they couldn't find a sponsor for a show featuring a black singer. The executives at NBC continued the show for over a year without a sponsor, operating at a loss. It was finally Nat who chose to discontinue the broadcast.[41]

Regardless, the show offered Americans an opportunity to invite Nat King Cole into their living rooms once a week to enjoy his music. The wall separating the races disappeared on the television screen. The American public had already gotten used to inviting the big bands, black and white into their homes by radio a generation prior. Nat King Cole's voice was so beautiful that it lifted the human spirit to a higher level where prejudice and bigotry couldn't survive. The messages of the songs were so universal that no one was excluded from delighting in the lyrics. The combination of words, melody, and voice along with Nat King Cole's warm, sincere personality were a force that allowed people to ignore any doubts or fears they may have had regarding racism.

White Americans were very comfortable gathered at the television admiring a black singer. African Americans were inspired by the talent of this great singer, and more than a little aware that Nat was making the world a better place. And once again, black and white came together. The white officials at NBC and the person of Nat King Cole joined forces to give the country some beautiful music. As a by- product of their efforts another mile of the road to integration was paved.

By the time of Nat King Cole's show, just about every American had already been watching *The Ed Sullivan Show.* Ed Sullivan, born in 1901, became a boxer, then a sportswriter, and then a Broadway newspaper columnist. In 1948 the CBS network hired him to host a variety show originally called *Toast of the Town* and then *The Ed Sullivan Show.* The impact that this show had on American culture, especially musical culture, was immeasurable and has not been duplicated since it went off the air in 1971. For twenty-three years Ed Sullivan presented every kind of music: classical, rock, jazz, blues, gospel, folk, popular, Broadway, opera—performed by males, females, blacks, whites—Ed knew no boundaries. Before the first show aired, Ed had a vision. In an interview he commented:

"The most important thing is that we've put on everything *but bigotry.* When the show first started in '48, I had a meeting with the sponsors. There were some Southern dealers present and they asked if I intended to put on Negroes. I said yes. They said I shouldn't, but I convinced them I wasn't going to change my mind. And you know something? We've gone over very well in the South. Never had a bit of trouble."

Ed Sullivan gave the American public the opportunity to enjoy all styles of music in all colors.

Without breaking any laws Ed Sullivan broke into almost every house in America and allowed Americans to experience the pleasure of a world without racial walls for one hour every Sunday night. This technological therapy was producing results not measured by the ratings or any sociological surveys.

The evidence that music was creating a different racial experience was easily seen on a TV show known as *American Bandstand*, whose broadcasts of rock & roll brought black culture into the world of white teenagers of the 1950s. Through the efforts of its host, Dick Clark, integration was a phenomenon that seemed perfectly natural. "Seamless" was the word Clark used to describe the process by which he introduced African Americans into the format. The twenty million teenagers who watched *American Bandstand* were being entertained in an integrated environment that to them seemed perfectly normal.

Like Ed Sullivan, Dick Clark didn't have to ask Congress to pass a law to get his show integrated. He spoke to the producers and advertisers. They apparently agreed with him that the time was right and that integration made sense and would succeed.

Gregory Salvatore Scime

Like Benny Goodman twenty years earlier, Dick Clark decided to integrate his area of music. By so doing he helped to create a whole generation of Americans who would not be looking at the world divided into black and white. Dick had the wisdom to know that no one could stop him from doing what he knew was right. As long as he could find financial backing for his show, and as long as he had a loyal audience, he knew that he didn't need permission from a group of legislators.

Chapter 9
My Soul's Been Anchored in the Lord

Music for the Soul of an Integrated Society

As rock & roll in the late1950s was evolving, the style was becoming less reflective of its R&B, blues, and gospel roots. Many black musicians didn't like where rock & roll was going, musically speaking, and wanted music that more closely reflected the African American experience. Somewhere, or everywhere, the energy and inspiration for a new musical expression was working its way through the black community looking for the right spokesperson who could find the right words and the right notes to bring this expression into existence.

In a relatively short period of a few years at least fifty people answered the call and three record companies responded to the need. This new form of musical expression was called "Soul." Like its predecessor, Rock & Roll, Soul had two distinctive styles. Whether it was the style of music coming from Stax Records in Memphis, Tennessee or the style coming out of Motown Records in Detroit, Michigan, all of the music came out of the black experience. But musically it was as different as James Brown and the Fifth Dimension. In every case, though, the different styles, no matter where you think they came from, all came from the experience of musicians growing up in the black church.

Originally, or so it was said, soul was supposed to be the sole possession of the black music world. The music—along with the hair styles, the food, the clothes, the walk and the talk—was supposed to be a rally cry for blacks at the beginning of the civil rights movement of the 1960s. But whether in the recording studio, or the front office, whether it was the singers or the composers, or the guitarists and the bass players, the line that was not supposed to be crossed couldn't be found. The "No Whites Allowed" sign had been removed from the world of black music. The civil rights movement was over in the world of music. Integration had reached the point of no return.

In the world of soul music it was record producer Berry Gordy leading the way. Only a few years prior Gordy had served in the army during the Korean War. Korea was the combat testing ground for integration in the armed forces. It would not have escaped a man of Gordy's intelligence that integration could be easily accomplished, as it had been in the military, if it were "task oriented."

The music was supposed to be a coded message for the black community. But the white younger generation broke the code and was enjoying the music as if it were their own. Older people didn't care about the code. They were simply taken in by the beauty and sophistication of the Motown sound and the rebellious—reminiscent of rock & roll—sound of the Memphis style.

Through this music black culture was being disseminated. The public was very comfortable with the manner in which the Motown artists presented themselves. Motown president, Berry Gordy, demanded that anyone representing his record company was groomed for public appearance. He made his performers dress, walk, talk, and act with class in public. The public was very comfortable with Berry's vision. The music was universal in its appeal.

The world was buying into the music. If the production of the music or access to the music required integration, then so be it!

For example, when the gospel, R&B, soul, and pop singer Sam Cooke refused to play to a segregated audience in Memphis, the KKK could only stand by and wonder. They had to be wondering why music fans were so willing to integrate themselves at a concert. It took thousands of National Guard troops to enforce integration in the schools of Little Rock in 1957. A few years later, however, it only took an army of one, Sam Cooke, to integrate the audiences at his concerts, even if these concerts were in the South. Cooke knew that the wall was there. He also knew that the beauty of the music, like Joshua's trumpets at Jericho, was going to take down that wall.

The success of soul was in no small part due to the work of many previous black singers. The "soulful" sound of

Nat King Cole and Johnny Mathis had further undermined resistance in the white community. People who grew up listening to Johnny Mathis were not concerned with his color. The adults of the 1950s who grew up listening to Nat King Cole in the forties had much the same feeling. Frank Sinatra's work toward integration was highlighted by his television show in the early 1950s. His frequent guests included black vocalists Ella Fitzgerald, Sammy Davis, Jr., and Lena Horne. When he sang duets with these great African American singers he was saying to the viewers, "There's nothing wrong with this. You should try it."

Two other white baritones of the 1950s, Perry Como and Bing Crosby, were using their movie and television careers to show their enjoyment performing with black musicians. The interaction of these men and women on television or in movies was a powerful lesson on integration. Yet, so subtle, no one at the time realized what they were learning.

Without breaking any laws the great singers of the 1940's and 1950's, black and white, were breaking down the mistrust and the misunderstanding between the two races. Listening to the voices of Nat King Cole, Ella Fitzgerald, and the many others was like a religious experience that left no room for hatred. Blacks and whites across the country were glued to their televisions week after week taking in the music and at the same time getting used to the image of blacks and whites enjoying each other's company.

Chapter 10
Who'll Be a Witness

Umpire and Role Model Emmett Ashford

When Thurgood Marshall was appointed as the first black Justice of the Supreme Court, the event, in 1967, was almost anticlimactic. One year earlier another black was appointed to a much more important judicial position; more important, at least, to the average American.

Emmett Ashford became the first black umpire in professional baseball in 1951 in the Southwestern International League. To many people it was becoming apparent that racial prejudice in baseball was on a downward spiral. In 1955, when Ashford was a guest on a television show hosted by Groucho Marx, Groucho is quoted as saying "I predict that you're gonna be in the big leagues within a year." He was referring the Major League Baseball. His prediction was off by only a few years. In 1961 Ashford was hired by the American League and by April 11, 1966, he was umpiring a major league baseball in Washington, D.C., between the Washington Senators and the Cleveland Indians. Groucho was a comedian, but he wasn't joking when he spoke of Emmett's future. His prediction was based on what he was seeing happening all over the country in the 1950's.

Known for his flashy style and impeccable dress, Emmett was entrusted with decision-making powers that, in the minds of millions of baseball fans, had more of an impact on everyday life than the opinions coming from the "Bench" of the Supreme Court in Washington. Emmett earned a reputation for being a good umpire. But there is no denying that Emmett, who was just being himself, brought excitement to role of the umpire. He umpired with a flair that (almost) everyone loved. The fans would frequently cheer for him as took the field. On one occasion a stadium announcer apologized to the fans that Emmet would be umpiring third base and therefore would not be behind home plate calling balls and strikes. And after a game it was not uncommon for younger fans to wait on line to get Emmett's autograph.

When Emmett became the first African American professional umpire in 1951 he may or may not have been aware that in less than one generation baseball would be completely integrated. The only exception was in the position of "manager." But even that was eventually remedied.[42]

To those people who in 1951 had a vision for the game of baseball it was probably apparent that the road to complete integration was under construction. The owners, managers, and players acted with integrity and a love of the game.

The willingness of white baseball fans to empower an African American with the authority to stand behind home plate and make decisions that would determine the outcome of a game was an indication that racial prejudice in baseball was eliminated. It was also an indication that attitudes about race had moved dramatically in a positive direction.

Chapter 11
I Got a Home in That Rock

Classical Music Opens Its Doors to Singers of All Races

In the world of classical music there are two primary categories, opera and instrumental music. The most important opera house in the United States is the Metropolitan Opera House at Lincoln Center in Manhattan, the borough of New York City that is built upon bedrock.

Throughout the 1950s and 1960s changes were taking place in the world of opera that mirrored events in the world of popular music. These two decades saw the rise of three important pioneers in the integration of the Metropolitan Opera House (after the brief appearances of Marian Anderson and Robert McFerrin.) Leontyne Price, George Shirley, and Martina Arroyo. Before their success they shared several things in common. All three began their musical life in church, and all had planned on a career in education.

Leontyne Price was born in Mississippi in 1927. Technically she was the first African American to sing with the Met, preceding Marian Anderson by two years when she sang George Gershwin's "Summertime" for a Metropolitan

Opera fund-raising event in 1953. Her first opportunity to perform on the stage of the Met came in 1959. She turned down the offer because it was only for a single performance of the opera *Aida*. But two years later, in 1961, she was offered an extended contract.

Born in Indianapolis in 1934, George Shirley was the first African American tenor to receive a contract from the prestigious Metropolitan Opera. He graduated with a music education degree from Wayne State University and was the first black member of the U.S. Army Chorus, where he was encouraged by fellow members to pursue a career in opera. Shirley took their advice and two years later, in 1961, won the Metropolitan Opera Auditions, which launched him on an eleven-year career with the prestigious opera company. Robert McFerrin, who had been an inspiration to Shirley, preceded him at the Met. But Shirley was the first African American tenor to sing leading roles there on an ongoing basis—performing twenty-eight different roles in twenty-six operas.

Martina Arroyo, born in Harlem in 1936, became famous for her interpretations of Verdi, Puccini, and Strauss. Working first as an educator and social worker, she began her Met career in 1958 by winning the Met's *Audition of the Air*. It was several years later that Martina received a phone call from Rudolf Bing, the general manager of the Met. He asked her to fill in for one of the world's most famous sopranos, Birgitt Nilsson. Arroyo went on to have a successful international opera career.

Although it was apparent as these singers were growing up in the 1930s and 1940s that they had extraordinary voices, Price, Shirley, and Arroyo may have assumed that the world of opera in America would not offer them any opportunities at the highest level, the racially segregated stage of the Metropolitan Opera.

These singers did not know that during this time that Sol Hurok, who was to become America's most important impresario and Marian Anderson's manager, had left Russia because of prejudice against Russian Jews. They did not know that in Nazi Germany a young Jewish man by the name of Rudolf Bing was being driven out of his birth country by the increasing prejudice against Jews, and would eventually migrate to the United State to become the General Manager of the Metropolitan Opera. They did not know that these two emigrants from the East would meet in the West and decide that prejudice against blacks had no place at the Met. Bing was especially determined to open the door of the Met to African Americans. Hurok was determined to have Marion Anderson walk through that door.

In 1955 Marian Anderson became the first African American to perform with the Met, but her performances there were few—nonetheless they were enough to convince the opera public that beautiful voices come in all colors. When Martina Arroyo, Leontyne Price, and George Shirley eventually made their entrance on the stage of the Met, they did what other great singers in the pop and jazz field did. They took their audience out of the real world into the beauty of a world created by Puccini, Verdi, and Mozart. By late 1961 the audiences at America's most elite musical venue were well into the evolutionary process of being cured of prejudice. Music was their therapy.

Similar opportunities were opening up for classically trained black instrumentalists and conductors, starting with the military.

At the end of World War II the army and navy left tens of thousands of troops in Germany, Japan, and at least a dozen other war-torn regions to stabilize the country and help with the rebuilding. The army had learned from the experience of James Reese Europe (see chapter 3), who during World War I taught the French to love American music, that important military outposts like Germany, Italy, and Japan required a first-class band for the purposes of public relations. So they set about to repeat this effort.

Shortly after Henry Lewis, an African American double-bass player, was drafted into the army in 1954 at the age of 22, he was sent to Germany to conduct the Seventh Army Symphony. To appoint Henry Lewis to such an important position, the army must have considered him to be a first-class musician and a first-class soldier.

For many young musicians, black or white, the army offered the extraordinary opportunity to hone their musical skills. Although Lewis had set as one of his goals the breaking down of racial barriers in the world of music, the army could not offer him the opportunity to pursue this goal—only because, by 1954 when Lewis was drafted, the armed forces were completely integrated. The best he could do in Germany was to develop his conducting skills. Apparently he did just that. A few years after he was discharged from the army he was appointed Assistant Conductor of the Los Angeles Philharmonic Orchestra under Zubin Mehta.

America came to yet another realization: talent for conducting has no racial requirements. And to the surprise of many, the all-white musicians of one of America's most important orchestras were perfectly willing to pick up their bows and play with little or no regard to the color of the conductor.

In the same year that Marian Anderson made her debut at the Met, 1955, a nine-year-old pianist won the Student Competition of the Philadelphia Orchestra. His name was André Watts. Andre was born in Germany to a Hungarian mother, Maria Gusmits, and an African American career soldier, Sergeant Herman Watts. At eleven years old Andre made his debut playing with the Philadelphia Orchestra in a performance of a piano concerto by the eighteenth-century composer Josef Haydn. People were being made aware that even among African America youth there was musical talent that wasn't limited to jazz.

In 1962 André Watts appeared as a soloist at Carnegie Hall with the New York Philharmonic conducted by Leonard Bernstein. When this concert was broadcast nationally in January of 1963, Americans, both black and white, were given the opportunity to see America's most important orchestra and America's most important conductor accompanying a completely unknown sixteen-year-old African American pianist performing the Franz Liszt Piano Concerto in E Flat, one of the most difficult pieces in the repertoire. (Watts was a last-minute substitute for well-known pianist Glenn Gould in this performance.)

It would be impossible to know the reaction that this performance was creating. But it would be safe to say that white Americans were surprised and impressed. Black Americans would not have been surprised by André Watts's talent, but no doubt they were proud and realized that another section of the wall had come down. And again the battle was won by an army of one person, who, at sixteen years old, was too young to enlist in the military.

It was clear in 1963 that the entire world of classical music, like jazz, pop and rock, had liberated itself from prejudice. And there was no way that the clock could be turned back. No one wanted it turned back; black musicians, white musicians, black teachers, white teachers—people of both colors ignored color when it came to music. Bigotry was no match for the power of Beethoven's music, or the music of Chopin or Puccini. The music, no matter who was playing it, or singing or conducting it, drove through every racial barrier like an M-1 tank through a picket fence.

As one obstacle after another was removed, bigotry was becoming something to be pitied, no longer feared.

Chapter 12
Rise, Shine, for Thy Light Is Coming

Black Political Leadership in the Late 20th Century through Today

When reveille sounded on August 9, 1989, Colin Powell woke up to the news that President George H. W. Bush was going to appoint him Chairman of the Joint Chiefs of Staff. Powell became the twelfth person to hold this position, but he was the first black to do so. When Powell was born in Harlem, N.Y., in 1937 the armed forces were segregated. A black officer would not have even been permitted into the officer's club.

When Powell joined the Reserve Officer's Training Corp as a college student in 1954 the armed forces had been desegregated. Only Colon Powell himself would have known what his aspirations were for his military career. Whatever they were, four presidents had their own aspirations for him.[43]

Upon recommendation, President Richard Nixon in 1972 chose Powell as a White House Fellow. The position was designed to offer selected individuals the opportunity to learn the working of government from the inside.

President Ronald Reagan appointed Powell as his National Security Advisor in 1987. Twenty years after Dr. Martin Luther King was considered a threat to national security, an African American was advising the president on who is and who isn't a threat.

The first President Bush appointed him Chairman of the Joint Chiefs of Staff in 1989. In just forty-one years the armed forces had so effectively desegregated that the highest-ranking military position was occupied by an African American.

Twelve years later, in 2001, the second President Bush, George W., appointed Powell as Secretary of State.

The appointment to Secretary of State put Powell in the public's eye on a regular basis. Although Powell had been considered presidential material before this appointment, it was this appointment that offered him an opportunity to demonstrate his potential. Although it hasn't happened in recent history, it is a fact that six men who held the position of Secretary of State went on to become president. There can be little doubt that President George W. Bush chose Powell to fill the most important cabinet post on merit. At the same time, however, the president had to be aware that Powell, who had already convinced everyone of his integrity and military leadership ability, would now be in a position to earn the trust of the American people. In fact, when Powell finished his term as Secretary of State he was probably the most trusted person in Washington.

When General Powell resigned his position in 2004 as Secretary of State at the end of Bush's first term, President Bush appointed another African American to take possession of the "Great Seal of the United States."* And this time it was an African American woman, Condoleezza Rice. Rice was not the first woman to hold this post, but she was appointed in the middle of America's biggest military conflict since Vietnam. Like Powell to President Reagan, Rice had been National Security Advisor to President George H.W. Bush. It is reasonable to assume that President Bush was looking for the best person for the job, not the best black person for the job. The days of racial identity at the highest levels of government were long gone.

To most people Condoleezza appeared to have come "out of the blue." It is not well known that her preparation for the position included being mentored, while she was teaching at Stanford University, by George Schultz, President Reagan's Secretary of State for seven years. Her entire career leading up to 2004 traveled a road that had few detours related to race. It was the same road Colin Powell had traveled. By the time Senator Obama threw his hat into the presidential ring he could see that the road to the highest position in Washington was safe to travel.

By 2007 the public was so used to having an African American in the highest cabinet post, at the president's side, that they began to think seriously about the possibility of an African American president. Powell's demeanor, maturity, and obvious wisdom made it easy for almost any American to picture him as president. Rice's performance in her international role made it easy for Americans to see a woman as president. Ethnicity and gender had become items of little importance in affairs of state.

Even the so-called tabloid newspapers couldn't get much traction with stories about Barack Obama's ethnicity when he was competing for the Democratic presidential nomination . In fact, there was very little public interest in the fact that fighting for the same nomination was a woman, Sen. Hillary Clinton. It all seemed perfectly normal. Both Democratic Party candidates were competing with each other and with the Republican candidates on a level playing field.

When Barack won the nomination you couldn't hear "a mumblin word" of complaint about his ethnicity. People challenged his youthful age, his lack of experience, some of his past associations, but his African American heritage was almost totally ignored. Senator John McCain, Obama's opponent in the final race, had no reason or desire to bring up race. No matter how often anyone tried to make race an issue, the subject matter fell on deaf ears. American voters were focused on some real problems. The people wanted "change" and "bi-partisanship." Both candidates promised to deliver on these requests. No one seemed to realize that the most important change had already been accomplished. Prejudice had been reduced to a manageable and perhaps an almost insignificant level.

The most important form of bi-partisanship was now in effect. People of different colors were working together for the common good.

Many people would say that Americans' prejudice was based on color. But it was not limited to color. Italians, Jews, Irish, and others were also subjected to prejudice, which can be attributed to fear, misunderstanding, and misjudgment on everything from skin color to religion, to different life-styles. There is a fear that someone who looks different might also think differently and have different values. African Americans like Jackie Robinson, Nat King Cole, Ella Fitzgerald, Louis Armstrong, and Colin Powell, to mention a few, demonstrated that shared values are not based on color. Without publicly talking about prejudice, they eliminated many of the primary causes of prejudice by simply doing what they did best, hit a baseball, sing a song, play the trumpet, lead an army. They had integrity that spoke to the heart, where truth is recognized first. Their accomplishments did not only affect the white population. All along the way, year after year, the majority of the black population was able to see the confirmation of that which they always knew about their own potential. Now this potential was being demonstrated, and recognized from every direction.

Not all white Americans were prejudiced. Those who spoke publicly about prejudice made it appear that all whites were irrationally bigoted all the time. It was not the reality. The majority of Americans were not feeling prejudice when they were being entertained with extraordinary music performed by extraordinary people. American baseball fans were not feeling prejudice when they watched Jackie Robinson steal home in the 1955 World Series. B-17 Bomber pilots were not feeling prejudice when the Tuskegee Airmen were escorting them through enemy skies during the World War II.

When Colin Powell became Secretary of State there was hardly a prejudiced voice left to complain. When Condoleezza Rice was appointed to succeed Powell in that position the complainers were at a loss as to what complaint they could come up with.

It was a journey of about a century and a half from the Emancipation Proclamation in 1862, to the Presidential Oath of Office 2008. It may seem to have taken a long time for the American way of life to become inclusive. The process, however, was very complex. It was not a simple case of writing a few laws and making everyone obey them.

First, there had to be a reason to integrate. The immorality of segregation was *not* something everyone agreed on. Integration is not one of the Ten Commandments. Jesus never mentioned it. Although slavery existed in the time of Jesus, there is nothing in the New Testament condemning slavery outright. Many people actually believed in their hearts that integration was wrong. Nevertheless, people were not going to integrate unless there was something to be gained.

Second, the process of integration, once a reason had been found, had to allow time for many factors to come together. A farmer plants in the spring, but nothing happens until the weather is warm enough and the moisture is right.

And even then it takes months to grow a simple tomato, because a tomato is not as simple as it looks.

Third, integration was not going to happen in every area of life at the same time. It would have been a shock to the culture. And it could not have taken root without the right conditions and the right people. Superficial changes, after some initial success, would have quickly failed. Integration that was engineered by self-serving leaders would not have brought about real progress.

Even when people were able to recognize the value of integration they needed to see it succeed in one area before moving on to the next. It would have been confusing to blacks and whites to see integration happening in every aspect of their lives at the same time. Even for those who would benefit the most, the process had to be in stages to allow for the necessary adjustments. Like removing an aggressive cancer with surgery and chemotherapy, prejudice had to be cured in stages. Like chemo, the cure for prejudice had to involve the right medicine in the right dosage at the right time.

Fourth, the right people had to be in the right place at the right time. If John Hammond had not introduced Benny Goodman to Teddy Wilson, and if Benny Goodman had not admired Teddy Wilson's piano playing, and if the technology of recording had not been invented, allowing the two men to perform together without being seen, and if the musical combination of these two musicians had not been perfect, and if those two men had not had the common bond of music, then we may have had to wait many more years for jazz to integrate.

If Sol Hurok had been less persistent, and if Eleanor Roosevelt had been out of town, and if Marion Anderson had not wanted to pursue the matter (because her career was already going well), then nothing would have happened on Easter Sunday morning in 1939 at the Lincoln Memorial in Washington, D.C.

If Branch Rickey had chosen someone other than Jackie Robinson, if Dodger fans were not tired of waiting for a World Championship, if the mood of the country had not been changed by World War II, then it might have taken another generation to integrate baseball.

If FDR did not have the vision for black aviators, if Harry Truman had not been influenced by "Black Jack" Pershing, if there had been no major war to allow black soldiers and sailors to prove themselves, if the armed forces had not been experiencing serious shortages of manpower caused by segregation, Executive Order 9981 might not have been issued.

None of the people mentioned in this book had as their primary goal to change the way people think. Instead they were offering people the opportunity to feel differently for a few hours a day at the ballpark, or to let music communicate what words cannot. The military was not trying out a social experiment; it was trying to protect the country in the most effective way. But the by-product was usually the same, people were changed.

Integration succeeded in music, baseball, and the military for many reasons. One reason is that the initiators of integration in those areas of life were not accusing anyone of being prejudiced. Another reason, they realized that what they wanted to do, where they wanted to do it, when they wanted to do it, and that the reasons for doing it were right. And miraculously they realized there was nothing to stop them.

The greatest advances in integration were achieved through cooperation, not confrontation. Race riots, like those in Chicago (1919), Tulsa (1921), and Detroit (1943) produced many casualties but few results. On the other hand, there were no riots or casualties while baseball achieved complete integration in thirteen years. There were no cross burnings or lynchings. There were, however, scores of fans cheering the achievements of athletes regardless of color. There were no riots while the same goal was being achieved in music in less than one generation. In fact, the audience at New York City's Metropolitan Opera House was applauding the arrival of Marion Anderson on stage before she opened her mouth to sing.

Complete integration in the Armed Forces was so uneventful that hardly anyone knows when it happened. For years army commanders actually asked some members of the press to refrain from reporting advances that the army was making in racially integrating military bases in the South. Racial bigotry in isolated incidents lingered for several years in the military after Truman's executive order. But by the mid-1950s these incidents were no longer commonplace.

It could be said that the period of 1935 until 1960 saw unprecedented progress in integration. During this period there were no race riots of any significance. By 1960 integration was moving like a two-mile-long freight train, slowly and almost impossible to stop. A whole generation of Americans was coming of age; a generation that had grown up in a world with different from their parents; a generation that was going to attend integrated colleges and serve in a military that had no racial barriers separating whites from blacks.

Yet race riots in the mid-1960s, beginning in 1964, were commonplace. Thousands wounded, hundreds killed, and in most cases riots were started by rumors. Neighborhoods were destroyed and could not recover. Perhaps it is the greatest irony in the story of American race relations that the most publicized efforts to achieve equality resulted in such widespread violence. Exploring the possible reasons behind this phenomenon would require another book, but suffice it to say that tolerance, and hopefully acceptance, must take place in the hearts of people and be given time to nurture before long lasting change can be achieved.

Baseball and music were like an antibiotic that enables the immune system to kill an infection. Prejudice is not natural to human beings. As composers Richard Rodgers and Oscar Hammerstein so effectively expressed in one of the songs from the Broadway musical South Pacific, in order to become prejudiced "You Have To Be Carefully Taught."

Baseball and Music enabled our spiritual immune system to eliminate this acquired disease, prejudice.

The corporate world was not far behind in creating a color-blind society. Business leaders in the 1940's saw integration in the workforce as profitable. They preferred to integrate voluntarily rather than by force of legislation. World War II made integration a necessity in the defense industry. As millions of American men were serving in the military, thousands of jobs opened up in the defense plants of the north. Companies like the Ford Motor Company were quick to learn that Blacks filled these vacancies quite effectively. The Ford Motor Company has a unique place in the economic history of black Americans. On the eve of World War II, Ford employed 10,000 black workers. (http://cliometrics. org/conferences/ASSA/Dec_90/Whatley-Wright_Abstract/)

Many of the writers of the Constitution knew that slavery was wrong. Although they could not specifically eliminate slavery through the Constitution at the time because of the views of the Southern states, they knew that it was only a matter of time before the country would find slavery unacceptable. The Constitution was carefully worded in a way that would allow future generations to interpret it to mean that second class citizenship was illegal.

In the years leading up to 1960, models of integration were appearing in every area of American society. By 1961, when the last professional sports team, the football Washington Redskins, integrated, racial integration in America had enough momentum in the every direction to eventually encompass the entire country and every aspect of life. Even professional hockey was briefly integrated in 1959 and again in 1961.

By 1960 bigotry in America was singing its Swan Song. Because it is a defect of human nature bigotry cannot be one hundred percent eradicated. Like bad weather, crab grass and unemployment there will always be racism. What matters is "how much?" By 1960 racism was brought under control and was no longer totally obstructing the lives of African-Americans. For African Americans in 1960 if one door was closed, another was open.

Discrimination is not something that ended on a particular day with passing of a particular law. Every time an African American man, women or child overcame an obstacle to achieve their goal they removed another brick from the wall and used that brick to build the road that others could follow.

When James Meredith, an African American. tried to enroll in the University of Mississippi in 1963 he was refused admission. Meredith was a nine year veteran of the U.S Air Force before applying to the university. He knew that he was on a one- man mission to integrate a bastion of segregation. And somehow he knew he would be assisted by his "brothers in arms," the U.S military, when he attempted to open the main gate of "Ole Miss" to African Americans. It only took eleven days to open the gate that had been closed to African Americans for one hundred nineteen years.

America was no longer tolerating the intolerant.

No Man Can Hinder Me

By 1960, in all fields of life, enough doors were opened that the pursuit of happiness was a reality for everyone.

By 1960 America elected its first Catholic president.

By 1960 the country was ready for the birth of the man who would become its first African American president.

Without making any laws or breaking any laws, integration in Baseball, Music and the Military was accomplished quietly, quickly and permanently, by men and women, black and white, who let no one hinder them.

Appendix

Louis Armstrong
The name Louis Armstrong is synonymous with the development and evolution of jazz. Most jazz musicians would agree that Louis was the greatest jazz musician of all time.

Louis claimed that he was born on July 4, 1900. Whether this is true or not, his contribution to American life would have earned him the right to have been born on such an important day.

Louis was an African American born in New Orleans. Deserted by his parents when he was young he was "kind of" adopted by a Jewish immigrant family by name of Karnofsky. It was the Karnofsky's who fed him, gave him a place to sleep, and it was the head of the family, Morris Karnofsky, who helped Louis buy his first cornet. The Karnofsky's recognized that Louis had talent and they encouraged him to pursue music. The life and contributions to music and integration of Louis are too important to be included as a only chapter in any book.

Endnotes

1   The phrase "African American experience" is used here with the understanding that although blacks in different groups throughout different parts of the country have experienced life in different ways, they have shared enough common ground (especially the encounter of racial prejudice) for this term to have validity.

2   Born in 1828 in Livingston County, New York, Clinton Bowen Fisk was an American soldier, abolitionist, businessman, and educator. On March 3, 1865, the Freedmen's Bureau Bill became law, sponsored by the Republicans to aid freedmen and white refugees. A federal bureau was created to provide food, clothing, fuel, and advice on negotiating labor contracts. It attempted to oversee new relations between freedmen and their former masters.

3   The American Missionary Association (AMA) was a Protestant-based abolitionist group founded on September 3, 1846, in Albany, New York. The main purpose of this organization was to abolish slavery, to educate African Americans, to promote racial equality, and to promote Christian values. Its members and leaders were of both races and chiefly affiliated with Congregationalist, Methodist, and Presbyterian churches.

4   See www.fisk.edu/.

5   A brief history of the Fisk Jubilee Singers can be found at www.fiskjubileesingers.org/our_history.html.

6   A full description of the way George Pullman created a middle-class black population is described in the book *Rising from the Rails* by Larry Tye. It is interesting to note that Supreme Court Justice Thurgood Marshall was the son of a Pullman Porter.

7   *Harlem's Hellfighters*, Stephen L. Harris.

8   Robinson at the time was a famous tap dancer who later became a star of film and stage. He served as a rifleman in World War I with New York's 15th Infantry Regiment, National Guard. As well as serving in the trenches in WWI, Robinson was also the 369th "Hellfighters Band" drum major. For more information on Bill "Bojangles" Robinson, see http://minglecity.com/group/knowledgeisking/forum/topics/bill-bojangles-robinson-king.

9   The Won Cause, pg 193 Barbara Gannon.

10 During the 1920s and into the 1930s the separation between blacks and whites extended even to the musicians. Bands were all white or all black.

11 It may have been Jazz producer John Hammond who introduced Goodman to Wilson.

12 See http://tpmsband.blogspot.com/2011/02/benny-goodman-teddy-wilson-gene-krupa.html.

13 Carnegie Hall was built by industrialist/philanthropist Andrew Carnegie. Carnegie also helped Booker T. Washington, a dominant figure in the African American community in the early twentieth century, create the National Negro Business League and was a major benefactor to The Tuskegee Institute. In 1903, as a gift

to the endowment fund of Tuskegee Institute, Carnegie gave $600,000 in the form of corporate bonds from his company, U.S Steel. This was in addition to annual gifts of $10,000 that Carnegie gave to the school.

14 "Stompin' at the Savoy" is a 1934 jazz standard composed by Edgar Sampson. It is named after the Savoy Ballroom.

15 The Lindy Hop is an American social dance, from the Swing dance family. It evolved in Harlem, New York City, in the 1920s and 1930s and originally evolved with the jazz music of that time. Lindy was a fusion of many dances that preceded it or were popular during its development but is mainly based on jazz, tap, breakaway, and Charleston. It is frequently described as a jazz dance. See http://en.wikipedia.org/wiki/Lindy_Hop.

16 Carnegie Hall has a seating capacity of 2760.

17 Eleanor Roosevelt, letter to Mrs. Henry M. Robert, Jr., Daughters of the American Revolution, February 26, 1939, Franklin D. Roosevelt Presidential Library and Museum. See http://docs.fdrlibrary.marist.edu/tmirhfee.html

18 According to one source (www.library.upenn.edu/exhibits/rbm/anderson/hurok1.html), "Sol Hurok may be credited not only with shaping the course of Marian Anderson's career but also with providing the counsel and care that allowed her to concentrate on singing rather than issues of politics, race, finances, and related details that are necessary to a concert career but debilitating to the study and practice of song."

19   http://miscbaseball.wordpress.com/2010/11/07/a-report-of-jackie-robinson-signing-with-the-brooklyn-dodgers.

20   This story is also told in Barber's 1982 book, *1947: When All Hell Broke Loose In Baseball.*

21   http://en.wikipedia.org/wiki/Buzzie_Bavasi.

22   Eight members of the participating White Sox including pitchers Eddie Cicotte and Claude (Lefty) Williams, outfielders Joe Jackson and Happy Felsch, first baseman Chick Gandil, shortstop Swede Risberg, third baseman Buck Weaver and reserve infielder Fred McMullin were all charged with conspiring to fix the outcome of the Fall Classic (World Series) against the Cincinnati Reds.

23   http://www.peeweereese.com/biography.htm.

24   Ibid

25   Earl Francis Lloyd was drafted the same year. Nathaniel "Sweetwater" Clifton, who played with the Harlem Globetrotters, had previously signed a contract to play with the NY Knickerbockers but not as a result of being drafted.

27   The Polo Grounds was a stadium in the borough of Manhattan in New York City. The center field wall was 480 feet from home plate.

28   Mitchell became their first player as a result of player drafts and trades.

29   In his book, *All That We Can Be,* co-authored with John Sibley Butler, Moskos writes, "This shaped experience helped instill in those who served, as in the national culture generally, a sense of unity and moral seriousness that we would not see again—until after September 11, 2001." He wrote in a November 2001

article in *Washington Monthly* (with Paul Glastris), "It's a shame that it has taken terrorist attacks to awaken us to the reality of our shared national fate."

30   Roosevelt, Theodore; ed. by Archibald Roosevelt (1968). *Theodore Roosevelt on Race, Riots, Reds, Crime.* Probe. p. 13.

31   //blog.aurorahistoryboutique.com/president-theodore-roosevelt-invites-booker-t-washington-to-dinner/.

32   Surprisingly, this was not Booker Washington's first visit to the Whitehouse. It was he, in fact, who in 1898 went to the White House to invite President McKinley to visit Tuskegee Institute when the president was to be in Georgia for the Atlanta Peace Jubilee.

33   *New York Times*, November 4, 2008.

34   Baseball legend Jackie Robinson actually faced court martial charges for refusing to move to the back of a military bus during World War II. Robinson refused because he knew that the army had desegregated the bus line that was involved—but the driver was unaware of this. Nevertheless, certain top-ranking officers misinterpreted Robinson's behavior. Robinson was eventually court-martialed and found innocent by a panel of nine white officers.

35   Lear had served with Gen. John "Black Jack" Pershing in the Spanish American War, the Philippine American War, and World War I.

36   See Martin Blumenson, *Eisenhower* (Ballantine Books Inc.: New York, 1972).

37   Irving Berlin (May 11, 1888–September 22, 1989) was born in Russia, where his family had experienced the revival of the pogroms. Berlin was young, but he

remembered watching his house burn to the ground during one bout of anti-Jewish rioting. Like other Russian Jews who migrated to America, Berlin was not a fan of prejudice. He is perhaps best known for having written "God Bless America."

38 *This Is the Army* began life as a Broadway musical designed to raise money for the military. It then toured the nation, and later the world, and was eventually made into a movie, starring the handsome young Lt. Ronald Reagan.

39 http://www.digitalhistory.uh.edu/historyonline/integrating.cfm.

40 Eisenhower himself did not believe that school segregation was necessarily wrong. But he knew that the Constitution did not allow it. First and foremost Eisenhower was a soldier. If the Constitution ordered integration, he was going to carry out those orders. Thirteen years prior Eisenhower was in charge of the D-Day landing in France. During the invasion and subsequent landings in France, "Ike" had the opportunity to command the black troops involved in the campaign. Documents show that he found their service to be "meritorious" (Memo, "Negroes in the Armed Forces", ca. 1945. White House File, Nash Papers).

41 Although jazz pianist and singer, Hazel Scott, in 1950 was the first African American to have her own TV show, Nat King Cole is more often given that distinction. This is probably due to the infancy of television in 1950.

42   In 1975 Frank Robinson became the first African American to be hired as a manager when the Cleveland Indians appointed him as player-manager.

43   Powell described joining the Reserve_Officers'_Training Corps (ROTC) during college as one of the happiest experiences of his life; discovering something he loved and could do well, he felt he had "found himself." Cadet Powell joined the Pershing Rifles, the ROTC fraternal organization and drill team begun by General John Pershing. See www.wikipedia.org/wiki/ Colin_Powell.

Bibliography

Bordman, Gerald. *An American Musical Theatre*. New York: Oxford University Press, 1978. Print.

Brokaw, Tom. *The Greatest Generation Speaks: Letters and Reflections*. New York: Random House, Inc., 1999. Print.

Brown, Charles T. *The Art of Rock and Roll*. Englewood Cliffs: Prentice-Hall, 1983. Print.

Clinton, Catherine. *The Black Soldier: 1492 to the Present*. Boston: Houghton Mifflin Company, 2000. Print.

Fletcher, Tony. *All Hopped Up and Ready to Go: Music from the Streets of New York 1927-77*. New York: W.W. Norton & Company, Inc., 2009. Print.

Garner, Joe *And The Crowd Goes Wild*. Sourcebooks, Naperville, IL 1999

Gates, Henry Louis, Jr. *Colored People: A Memoir*. New York: Vintage Books, 1994. Print.

Harris, Stephen L. *Harlem's Hell Fighters: The African-American 369th Infantry in World War I*. Washington, D.C.: Brassey's Inc., 2003. Print.

Gregory Salvatore Scime

Keil, Charles. *Urban Blues*. Chicago: The University of Chicago Press, 1966. Print.

Larson, Arthur. *Eisenhower: The President Nobody Knew*. New York: Charles Scribener's Sons, 1968.   Print.

Martin, Henry. *Enjoying Jazz*. New York: Schirmer Books: A Division of Macmillan, Inc., 1986. Print.

Moskos, Charles C. and Butler, John Sibley. *All That We Can Be: Black Leadership and Racial Integration the Army Way*. New York: The Twentieth Century Fund, Inc., 1996. Print.

Nelson, Peter N. *A More Unbending Battle: The Harlem Hellfighters' Struggle for Freedom in WWI and Equality at Home*. New York: Basic Civitas Books, 2009. Print.

Nichols, Lee. *Breakthrough on the Color Front*. New York: Random House, Inc., 1954. Print.

Robinson, Rachel with Daniels, Lee. *Jackie Robinson: An Intimate Portrait*. New York: Abrams, 1996. Print.

Sasser, Charles W, *Patton's Panthers*. Pocket Books a division of Simon & Schuster New York 2004

Seay, Davin with Neely, Mary. *Stairway to Heaven: The Spiritual Roots of Rock 'n' Roll*. New York: R a n d o m House, Inc., 1986. Print.

Shaw, Arnold. *The World of Soul: Black America's Contribution to the Pop Music Scene*. New York: Cowles Book Company, Inc., 1970. Print.

Southern, Eileen. *The Music of Black Americans: A History, third edition*. New York: W. W. Norton   and   Company, 1997. Print.

Southern, Eileen. *Readings in Black American Music, second edition*. New York: W. W. Norton and Company, 1983, Print.

Szatmary, David P. *Rockin' in Time: A Social History of Rock and Roll, sixth edition*. Upper Saddle River: Pearson Prentice Hall, 2007. Print.

Tye, Larry. *Rising from the Rails: Pullman Porters and the Making of the Black Middle Class*. New York: Henry Holt and Company, LLC, 2004. Print.

Yanow, Scott. *Afro-Cuban Jazz*. San Francisco: Miller Freeman Inc., 2000. Print.